BUSINESS
VALUATION
BLUEBOOK

Also by Chad Simmons:

The Anonymous Entrepreneur
12 Steps to Build the Entrepreneurial Attitude

BUSINESS VALUATION BLUEBOOK

How Entrepreneurs Buy, Sell and Trade

CHAD SIMMONS
The Corinth Press

First Edition
Library of Congress Catalog Card Number 00-132371
ISBN 0-9661923-2-X

Edited by Jane Doyle Guthrie
Printed in the United States by Mennonite Press

Published by
The Corinth Press
A Publishing Division of
Simmons Investment Company, LLC
4200 Somerset, Suite 245
Prairie Village, KS 66208

www.corinthpress.com

Note to the Reader

Entrepreneurs are lively pioneers who choose small businesses as their creative frontiers. By improving business profit and value they hope to achieve creative fulfillment and financial autonomy. Together these comprise the freedom offered by the American system of free enterprise.

Business value is a central issue for entrepreneurs as well as professionals who serve them. During the past 20 years I have been a small business broker, buyer, operator, seller, investor and consultant. In these capacities I have worked with bankers, lawyers, accountants, estate planners and others to help my clients and me succeed. In each case, business value emerged as a lynchpin of negotiation. As a result, business valuation skill has provided me with an important marketing differentiation. I have been able to move beyond "how" to "how much" my work affects value. You can do the same.

This book offers new information and perspective on business valuation. The techniques presented are ideally suited for the company with fewer than 50 employees but they can be used for much larger enterprises, too. In either case, my goal is to provide tools you can use *and* show you how to use them. Any occasion to employ business valuation skill has the potential to make or save you thousands. So, linking this fundamental knowledge to your dynamic world is both the challenge and signature of this book.

Use the material in this book at your own risk. It is provided for information purposes only. In all cases, readers are advised to seek the advice of qualified business professionals including (but not limited to) those offering tax, legal and accounting expertise. Neither the author, publisher nor related parties involved with the development or distribution of this book and related materials assumes any responsibility or liability for the consequences, good or bad, of your use of this information.

Finally, in the past 20 years many have contributed to the experience and information I've translated into this book. Some taught me a great deal. Others offered only a phrase – but one that was unforgettable. Instead of naming them all I encourage you to share this material with others. Passing this information forward assures the wisdom of my mentors is acknowledged and renews the circle of entrepreneurship in you.

Chad Simmons
April 2000

TABLE OF CONTENTS

Chapter 1
Successful Entrepreneurs Know Business Value

Many entrepreneurs succeed at the improbable task of building a business without knowing what it is worth. And a business might be the entrepreneur's largest investment. This phenomenon occurs among a majority of the nearly 22 million small businesses in America today. In the details that accompany launching, buying, managing and selling companies, measuring the overall result can be forgotten. Determining the value for shares of stock, a car, a boat or a home is easy by comparison – 10 minutes of research on the Internet or a call to a broker can produce a reliable result. It isn't the same with a business. Estimates of business value are difficult to find. But measuring the wealth they create is of equal or greater importance.

This text is about business valuation techniques that can be used by entrepreneurs. They are not designed to convert entrepreneurs into business appraisers, which is a specialty practiced by few. Business appraisers use procedures that are more complicated than the ones presented here. It can take years of effort and considerable cost to develop an appraiser's level of valuation skill. It is not surprising then that a good business appraiser is hard to find. The cost of an appraisal will reflect this imbalance of supply and demand, too.

Entrepreneurs do not want or need to become business appraisers. They should become good at evaluating the merits of an investment and knowing what it is worth – fast. Years of education to learn this skill may not be a realistic option. Moreover, given the size of many small businesses that change hands, the cost of a formal business appraisal is often a bigger solution than the problem needs. A point of diminishing return is quickly reached.

Entrepreneurs need business valuation techniques they can use to derive results that are reliable and accurate. Or they need professional representatives who can do so for them – bankers, attorneys, accountants, estate planners and brokers. Valuation is an empowering skill for anyone associated with businesses that are bought, built and sold. However, the cost/benefit relationship of business valuation is most favorable for entrepreneurs.

Types of Business Value

When reviewing literature pertaining to the world of business valuation, one thing becomes clear. Events that warrant a business valuation are frequently linked to a transfer of ownership, or its potential, in the path ahead. An entrepreneur's success or failure often depends on the ability to buy low and sell high. But how do you know where to place your bets? Those who win most know business value best.

Business valuation may be challenging because the same company can be valued several different ways to produce a variety of results. This is because a business functions on several fields of play. The estimate is influenced by the rules of each game:
- Estate planners value client businesses low to reduce estate taxes.
- Bankers value businesses low to limit risk when the business collateralizes a loan.

- Divorce attorneys value a business low or high depending on whom they represent.
- Business appraisers offer an unbiased opinion of value, but compare three appraisals on the same business. They are seldom the same.
- The IRS seems to value a business low when allowing depreciation deductions and high when it is sold (to produce a bigger capital gain).
- Entrepreneurs selling a business want the highest price they can get; a buyer wants the lowest.

Who is right and who is wrong? Values that accomplish the intended objective are accepted most often as correct, so a business can have many different ones at the same time. Use of value and quality of results it produces determine what valuation estimate is best.

With so many reasons to calculate value, one quickly discovers each professional has his or her own technique. With so many values available, a "value range" can be established for any business. Then the one appropriate for most uses will exist somewhere within the range.

Business liquidation value is at the low end of the value range and is purely market driven. Value here is the result of what the property can be sold for at auction. *Book value*, another type, is constructed from assets and liabilities. This appears in every financial statement. However, book value is considered very low and seldom recognized as an accurate representation of business market value.

At the upper limits of the value range one finds another example that is also market driven. *Momentum Value* is generated by a popular business concept, new technologies, impressive earnings forecasts and media attention that electrify investors. The perception of value becomes greater than the value determined from financial results. Prices can soar.

Benchmark business values, those best suited to the entrepreneur's buying and selling activity, are derived from factors intrinsic to the business. These are cash flow, assets, returns on investment and sales revenues. They exist as a range in the middle of the value range and are influenced but not driven by market forces. These benchmark values take into consideration the value of intangible assets, or intellectual capital, too. It is the total collection of assets deployed that builds a stream of business performance. This is extrapolated into business value using a healthy balance of objective analysis and perception.

Business intangible assets (intellectual capital) are what many ask about when they inquire, "What is the business goodwill worth?" Goodwill is created when business performance creates value that exceeds the fair market value of tangible assets. Goodwill is usually not as great as many think, or expect, and is created from the valuation formula – not added to the result. But there are exceptions.

One case where a business does not even exist but can attract a value to be paid for goodwill is the franchise. There are over 2,000 franchise companies operating in the United States. They utilize imitative entrepreneurship to create the goodwill they sell. One needs to look no farther than the success record of other franchisees to confirm this fact. Franchisers sell a proven method of business operation and a uniform identity that has proven desirable to a target market. The exchange for access to these resources is called a "franchise fee." This is essentially the investment a new franchisee makes in goodwill and does not include the associated costs of starting a business: location and building improvements, furnishings, fixtures, equipment and inventory. Nevertheless, the old axiom "To reduce risk, don't start a business that may fail when you can buy one that hasn't" applies equally to a franchise opportunity.

Business value is an estimate of what a business is worth and can run from one extreme to another. Values in this range have the potential to be correct at the right time and place. This text discusses valuation techniques that fit into situations most frequently experienced by the small business entrepreneur. That is the occasion to buy and sell.

The evidence reveals business valuation most often occurs out of a need to facilitate a change in business ownership. Here is the common ground among all who have interest in learning this skill. Accordingly, material presented throughout this text supports those professionals and entrepreneurs seeking to value businesses for this reason. Hence, the term "value" is used interchangeably with "price."

A Valuable Investment of Time

A knowledge of business valuation techniques can lead to an increase in productivity for the small business entrepreneur. Fortunately, not every valuation estimate needs to be extensive to provide a meaningful result. Indeed, the objective of this text is to reduce the time it takes to develop sensible estimates of business value. Million-dollar solutions are attractive but not necessary to produce a better result. The devil is in the details of discovery. Focused attention to this phase of valuation lays the groundwork for complex and simple valuation formulas. With good data, results from each type of valuation technique can be similar enough to be useful. The process does not have to be complicated … it just has to be good.

Business valuation skill saves time. Like most things, regular use improves efficiency. With practice it is possible to value businesses very quickly. Of equal importance, one discovers specific pieces of information are initial indicators of value for specific types of businesses. For example, in a restaurant, cost of goods expressed as "food cost" is important. If it is out of the range of 22% to 42%, something is amiss. Low food cost is attractive, possibly indicating a high value. High food cost is unattractive, or it could be an opportunity in disguise – a chance to reduce food cost and return the savings to earnings. That's a diamond in the rough. The ability to identify critical information and interpret it more quickly and correctly, results in a savings of the entrepreneur's time.

For some, valuation skill helps prevent time spent on properties not worth the attention. This is not to say all businesses don't have value. They do. Recognizing the right value is the secret. When a business is sold it includes income, assets and a marketing opportunity. The valuation process encourages a review of these things. Sometimes business income is not sufficient to justify a price that is greater than the market value of the assets. This means the business price will be based on assets. Other times there will be no income at all and no assets, but an exciting marketing opportunity. These businesses are a popular acquisition: a franchise. Recognizing that these components of value exist will help the valuation analyst target attention to discover and evaluate the source and size of business value.

Business valuation saves money. This occurs when professional representatives, brokers or entrepreneurs can estimate value themselves. The need to hire another to perform this function is eliminated. Valuations for businesses can be quite expensive.

The most obvious opportunity for business valuation to have a direct (and favorable) impact on entrepreneurs' wealth is when buying or selling a business. Good valuation skill reduces the possibility a business will be sold for too much or too little. For sellers there is a less chance a business will be sold under the market – they save money. For buyers there is a better chance they will not pay too much for a business – "You make your money when you buy – not when you sell." In either case, business valuation helps improve the professional and financial results.

Business valuation skill improves negotiating effectiveness, too. For example, a question such as, "How did you arrive at that value?" can completely disarm the unprepared or uninformed. A response to explain how value is developed can win this important debate. The solid base of logic used to develop value builds confidence, which offers the strength to more comfortably and favorably resolve issues of disagreement. Price is normally a centerpiece of any negotiation. Assuming both parties are equally motivated to make a deal, the side with the most logical basis supporting their position usually wins. Business valuation provides this distinct advantage.

Finally, time spent valuing businesses can translate into a very high income earned per hour. Here is a case in point. Average sales prices for businesses often exceed $250,000. With a 10% margin for negotiation, there is $25,000 to argue about. Assume it takes forty hours to perform a reasonably accurate business valuation. If the valuation helps build a case resulting in acceptance of a sales price of $225,000 the savings is $25,000. The entrepreneur's time spent developing this value is worth $625 per hour.

"Comps" Don't Always Compare

One doesn't have to proceed too far in a discussion of business valuation before rules of thumb from comparable sales show up. The premise, "form follows function," is used as a best defense. For example, if 10 bowling alleys sell for an average of $35,000 per lane, then the bowling center being discussed should sell for the same multiple. What if its revenue is half or double the revenue of those in the sampling from which the multiple was developed? The use of comparable sales is suddenly suspect.

Comparable business sales, otherwise known as "comps," are often regarded as a useful device to determine business value in the buying and selling game. This is very popular in the real estate business, too, where the value of a three-bedroom ranch-style home can be determined from the recently closed sale prices of similar homes in the same neighborhood. However, the opportunity to compare business sales is limited and less reliable. Key variables affecting this valuation strategy are similarity of businesses in the sampling, number of businesses in the sampling, their location and the age of sale data.

Multiples from comparable sales have merit if they are created from businesses that are similar to the one under study. This means similar revenue, earnings, cash flows and operating management almost never occur. The multiples are helpful as quick estimates of value but further investigation is required.

Size of sampling (number of comps) available to interpret business value is usually small. No two businesses are exactly alike with the same ownership, capital structure, management skill and market characteristics. Even franchisees, designed to follow a proven business strategy as precisely as possible, are not equal. Further, the number of businesses qualifying as similar enough is not large. It is difficult to capture a supply of business sales data that can be used to define consistent trends with a high degree of probability.

Location also affects the comparables sales when attempting to establish business value. To develop a larger database of comparable sales, many draw upon business sales data from other regions. Casting a wider net only means the holes in the net become larger. Data taken from markets with dissimilar economic characteristics means the businesses perform differently. This unfavorably affects the quality of the information. A frozen yogurt shop in Vail, Colorado, will fetch a higher price than the same business in Nowhere, Alaska. The "location, location, location" rule always applies and affects business value.

A third weakness in the use of comps to establish value is the age of sale data. The same motive that leads valuation analysis to seek information about sales in other locations causes them to accept information that is two, three or four years old. This type of dated information can be dangerous to use. Imagine using basic indicators of performance to value an e-commerce provider based on the companies in operation when the Internet was new. That world changed so rapidly, the value calculated would be very wrong today. Consider the effects of using comps from an area that experienced tremendous economic growth in tourism or, conversely, the layoff of thousands from major plant closings. Dated information can create inaccuracies in business value.

Where comps can be helpful is when their internal operating ratios are used as a device for comparison. Suppose a survey of 50 restaurants with $500,000 to $1 million in revenue reveals the average food cost is 35%. This can be helpful to determine how a restaurant under study compares – favorably or unfavorably. But it is not a direct indicator of business value. There are many sources for this type of information that can assist the analyst becoming familiar with operating characteristics of specific business types. They are not, however, strong indicators of value. Business value is better derived from existing financial barometers of performance and market characteristics. Comps may be used to help confirm the result but not create it.

Valuation for Do-It-Yourselfers

Most people believe business valuation techniques are difficult to learn and apply. The thickness and high cost of books on the topic tend to confirm this belief. Financial statements that provide key information only make matters worse for those with little or no exposure to accounting. However, competent business valuation is easier to learn than most realize. In fact, anyone with the ability to start, acquire, own or operate a business has all the intellectual horsepower needed. The process is actually very simple and includes four steps:

- Collect information.
- Interpret information.
- Reorganize information.
- Calculate the results.

What many discover is the fourth step, calculating the result, is the easiest part. The first three are more difficult because they depend on the analyst's understanding and experience. With practice both improve. A more difficult challenge, however, is finding ways to practice. Here are a few suggestions to accelerate the learning curve of business valuation.

First, make it relevant. It is harder to learn new concepts where there is no specific application. So find one and new skills come easier and faster. Apply the material in this text to a business already owned or acquisition candidates under review.

Second, stick to the basics. It is easy to get lost in the details of business valuation. The valuation formulas are designed to prevent this from happening. They guide the effort in the same way Albert Einstein used a dictionary to remember all the words he couldn't. The formulas reorganize information the preparer may already know so it has new meaning. A methodical approach achieves the best results in the least amount of time.

Third, keep intellect and integrity connected. Learning business valuation techniques is an empowering, exciting experience. Many immediately see its power to propel their entrepreneurial careers. Temper this newfound strength so it doesn't become a weakness. Some attempt to adjust key variables and manipulate value to suit their need. It can happen to such an extent value becomes a distorted reflection of the entrepreneur's desire and not an image of reality. That is counterproductive. By all means adjust variables to improve accuracy, but resist temptation to go too far.

Last, remember the value is just an estimate. Business values are a blend of many factors, consider them all in the analysis. It is easy to calculate a low or high business value, but it is of no use if there are no takers. The best sales value is found within a range. It is a well-constructed compromise of all the business characteristics. To build the range a knowledge of business valuation is required.

Chapter 2
Due Diligence – Research Basics to Learn Specifics

An investigation that describes a business for purposes of acquisition is often called a "Due Diligence Report" or a "due diligence." This report may be a brief summary or an extensive business review and is often accompanied by descriptive exhibits. In general, a due diligence process has two parts: discovery and interpretation.

Boundaries of a Due Diligence

Entrepreneurs must know what they are buying, selling or trading for other property. The due diligence supports this activity. It is also useful when securing financing for expansion or planning general business strategy, both are designed to improve profit. Taken a step further, the due diligence conducted to develop a business valuation is especially meaningful. A plan to increase profits by $10,000 could increase value by $50,000 or more.

Due diligence reports are prepared by business buyers, sellers, managers, independent business consultants, business or real estate brokers, bankers, accountants, attorneys, financial planners and anyone involved in business management and ownership transfers – the most frequent reason a due diligence is performed. Settling the question of price has major financial implications.

When conducting a due diligence, the analyst collects a variety of data describing the business and its record of performance. This is interpreted afterward and conclusions are summarized in a final report. As it may form the basis for an important decision to buy, sell or trade a business, the depth or detail of the process tends to increase in proportion to the value and commitment of money and resources.

The most frequently requested information for a due diligence precedent to a business valuation is three to five years financial statements or tax returns. But more information is also sought in follow-up requests. Following are examples of the type of materials often collected for the business valuation due diligence:

- Company identification
- Ownership structure w/shareholder agreements
- Business location and contact points
- Description of business activity
- Summary of trailing revenue, expenses and earnings
- Statement of the business capital structure
- List of business assets
- Market position of the business
- Description of products and services offered
- Characteristics of the workforce
- Marketing opportunities within reach
- Photographs, maps and descriptions of premises and key equipment

- Location analysis
- Competitive market analysis
- A multi-year forecast of business financial results

When a due diligence is being performed, the prevailing rule to follow is, "Whatever the analyst wants, the analyst gets."

Collecting information for the due diligence report occurs via meetings with business principals. They or their appointed representatives work closely with the analyst. These meetings expedite the due diligence/valuation process. Serious investors leave no stone uncovered in their inquiries. Good information helps reduce uncertainty and reduce business risk. If transactions become lengthy, updates to the due diligence are often requested.

Performing a due diligence for a small business valued under $5 million can be difficult. Information requested is private – not public – so access has always been strictly limited. Company contacts occur directly with business principals whose sense of exposure is professional and personal. Sensitive information inadvertently released to competitors or the wrong people can cause serious damage to business performance. Financial statements are a grade card of management performance and may reveal unsatisfactory marks. Therefore, it is natural for business owners to enter a due diligence with skepticism and concern.

Most business relationships begin with a high measure of threat which inhibits the due diligence process. Trust is built with frequent contact, consistency of purpose and diplomacy. Following are helpful tactics that will produce good due diligence results.

1. Follow country wisdom: "Spit and whittle" first.
2. Explain the due diligence process before beginning.
3. Offer a timetable for completion.
4. Provide a written description of information requested.

5. Ask easy questions first – more difficult questions later.
6. Periodically remind principals of the purpose for the due diligence.
7. Focus on how the report helps principals achieve their objectives.
8. Be candid, objective and listen more than talk.
9. Execute and deliver a confidentiality agreement to the principals.

Non-Disclosure Agreements

Non-disclosure agreements are written promises not to disclose confidential information about a business making such disclosures. General business information not considered sensitive or damaging may be released prior to execution of a non-disclosure agreement. However, the formal due diligence process will begin after a non-disclosure is in place.

Those interested in learning more about a specific business – buyers, brokers, accountants, lawyers, bankers, etc. – give a non-disclosure or confidentiality agreement to the business owners. It is a normal and appropriate procedure, necessary because maintaining secrecy while conducting a due diligence is imperative to all concerned. Non-disclosure agreements permit interested parties to quickly establish their legitimacy, discretion and reliability with business principals. It is a counterpoint to a seller's release of financial information as an indication of serious intent. Non-disclosure agreements are convenient vehicles to handle this issue briskly and with dexterity.

Non-disclosure agreements are no guarantee of secrecy, however. Unfortunately, business principals themselves are often the source of information leaks. Innocuous conversations with an employee, spouse or business associate may contain references that appear harmless but could be explosive. Once out of the ownership loop, "inside" information gets reinterpreted and can travel exceptionally fast. The mere mention that a due diligence is occurring may be enough to set imaginations and rumors in motion. These can demoralize employees and drive off customers. Conscientious attention to this issue by *all* parties is required to preserve confidentiality.

Non-disclosure agreements come in many forms. Some are literally an analyst's one-sentence promise not to tell what he or she learns. Others are pages of detailed instructions that converge at the point of remedies. These follow as additional pages of threats to be exercised if the promises kept are broken. Non-disclosure agreements typically include the following elements:

- Name of the party giving the promise (Often names the analyst conducting the due diligence and the clients if any.)
- Name of the party receiving the promise
- Statement of the confidentiality promise (Explains what the analyst promises to retain as confidential; i.e. types and formats of information released. Sometimes this is added as an exhibit to ensure specific areas are covered by the agreement while others remain off limits. For example, material pertaining to financial performance is available while material pertaining to product development is not. The decision to exclude certain information is most often governed by the intended use of the due diligence investigation.)
- Limitations on use of information received (States the purpose for receiving privileged information. The agreement may include a statement defining who, in addition to the analyst, may have access to information disclosed. If third-party advisers – a client, supervisor, accountant, banker, attorney, business consultant, investor or other professional representative – are involved, they may be asked to execute a separate but similar agreement. This will occur prior to receipt of any privileged information.)
- Breach of agreement (Defines acts that constitute a breach of the agreement – generally unauthorized releases of

confidential material.)

- Remedies for breach of agreement (Typically grants the party receiving the confidentiality agreement the legal right to secure relief and compensation from the analyst. It may include a provision for a restraining order and/or court injunction to prevent further release of potentially injurious information. It could also address the penalties for breach of the agreement that, in some cases, can include court costs to secure prevention of further release; cash penalties; or any other remedy legal counsel for the damaged party chooses to pursue in addition to court and legal costs of collection.)
- Term (Normally ties expiration to a date set after the due diligence is completed. One to two years is not uncommon.)
- Signature and date

Failure to Disclose

In some cases, despite the existence of a fully executed confidentiality agreement, business principals may elect to withhold certain information requested. This may be ownership's prerogative. Confidentiality agreements do not necessarily grant the analyst rights to demand information; they grant business principals the right to take legal action if information disclosed is not kept confidential. Still, failing to disclose relevant information can be a warning flag. It may also be counterproductive, as it prevents the analyst from conducting a due diligence in advance of a business valuation. Worse, it often creates suspicion that business principals are attempting to cover up problematic issues. Business buyers or their representatives will usually withdraw their interest when information is withheld. Thus, failure to disclose is a frequent deal killer.

The primary asset purchased with a business is usually the stream of income. Without financial records to describe it, neither broker nor buyer can know what is offered. Therefore, the broker is attempting to represent a property with benefits not available or evident – like trying to sell a property sight unseen.

The investor is attempting to buy it under the same conditions. Both make commitments of time and money to investigate a risk-filled venture without knowing if initial interest or effort is justified. Neither can calculate an initial estimate of value based on fact.

Perhaps more importantly, accountants or attorneys cannot properly advise the parties as to the size and scope of business implications created by a business transaction without detailed disclosures. Bankers will not consider financing any kind of business either without financial disclosures to justify and assure repayment of debt is plausible. The ability to repay it from business earnings must be clear and unquestionable. This is only possible when financial disclosures, limited while still revealing enough to engender increased interest, are made at the appropriate time – before the offer is made.

The non-disclosure agreement is a precedent to a due diligence. This comes before an offer to purchase a business that spells out the conditions of a sale. A contract contingency to permit more detailed disclosures after acceptance of an initial offer is the norm. Experienced brokers perform their due diligence when listing a property in anticipation of questions and inquiries that will follow. They know a client's follow-up investigation will occur to confirm specifics of representations.

Business owners who fail to disclose necessary information as part of a due diligence investigation are shortsighted. They immediately disqualify knowledgeable and capable players. The price paid is very often a business that does not sell, becomes shop-worn or becomes known as "on the market" over time. It can be weakened by competitors and eventually lose customers and business revenue. Ownership burnout often occurs, too. The final outcome may be liquidation for pennies on the dollar. Sadly, with a good due diligence/business valuation and reasonable expectations, such a business might have sold earlier for a profit.

Ensure business principals are cooperative and forthcoming with information needed by adding a failure to disclose provision to the confidentiality agreement. As a result, requested materials are easier to collect. If materials are not forthcoming, the analyst may be released from any continuing obligation to perform services.

Organizing a Due Diligence

Knowing what to ask for, when to ask for it and how to organize information will make a due diligence easier and more productive. It is helpful to recall two premises that prompt the effort: 1) Is information related to a specific event? (Does someone want to buy, sell, trade or refinance the business?) and 2) Is the due diligence related to a specific time? (How much time is going to be available to complete the task?)

Suppose owners of a restaurant were interested in financing to expand the kitchen production capacity – an event. Indicators needed for a quick feasibility estimate might include the following:

- Financial statements
- Existing mortgages or liens
- Leases for equipment and the location
- Current equipment list with descriptions of major machinery
- A three-year revenue/earnings forecast

This should be sufficient to construct a preliminary cost/benefit assessment of the proposed expansion strategy. If favorable, a more complete due diligence may be performed. From that, changes in business value may be estimated to measure the total benefit of the expansion plan. Sometimes adding $10,000 to earnings creates an additional $50,000 of business value – equity. Keep this in mind. Bankers want to know how much additional profit is created, but business valuation skill permits the entrepreneur to go farther by estimating wealth created through refinancing to support expansion.

Time is a factor when information is needed quickly. Perhaps an opportunity to acquire a competitor or accept an unsolicited offer is in play. The more likely approach to a due diligence in this case will begin with an all-out document dump. Everything comes at once and it is the analyst's job to quickly organize, prioritize and produce meaningful results.

The value of regular business valuations there cannot be overstated – opportunity comes unexpectedly. The ability to act fast (with homework already in place) provides a competitive advantage.

To simplify the reporting process, data may be prioritized in categories. This divides discovery into steps that match the results needed with the time and energy used to develop them. For example, restaurateurs are acutely aware of *food cost* (i.e., the cost of food purchased expressed as a percent of gross income). This data item offers a quick indicator of gross profitability. If the figure is low, management probably runs a tight ship; too high and there are probably old prices on the menu, excessive waste in the garbage at day's end or theft. This single measurement device provides valuable clues to the restaurant's overall operating efficiency. Determine this percentage of revenue first.

Follow up receipt of initial indicators of business performance by requesting key strings of more detailed data. This would be priority types of information from other categories within the due diligence inquiry. For example, food cost information is more meaningful when combined with traffic count at the existing location, seating capacity and service style, market position, promotional tactics, age of kitchen and equipment and menu selections. One or two descriptive sentences for each is often enough to determine if the property is worth a closer look. If not attractive move on, wasting little time.

To organize and prioritize information efficiently the following checklists (covering Finance, Control, Marketing, Sales Production and Service) may be helpful. The categories are common to all businesses, and the information listed can be selected on a case-by-case basis. Asterisked (*) items are most important; they help form a good early impression of the business with less due diligence.

Finance

1. Contact Persons (name, address, phone, fax and e-mail of each)
___Business principal*
___General manager
___In-house bookkeeper
___Certified public accountant
___Banking representative

2. Mortgages and Notes Payable
___Principal Balances*
___Term of loan/interest rate/payment amount
___Payoff date and penalties associated
___Collateral pledges
___Identity of persons signing and guaranteeing payment

3. Leases for Location and Equipment
___Description of location or materials covered by the lease
___Amount of lease payments due*
___Payment schedules
___Term of the lease and options to renew
___Responsibilities (who pays for what)

4. Accounts Receivables/Payables
___Amount of each*
___Separate each in to 30, 60, 90 and over 90 days due
___Historical record of changes in both
___Ratio of accounts receivables to accounts payable over time*
___Collection procedures
___Cash or accrual method of accounting used
___Estimate of revenue from work under contract but not performed*
___Estimate of work to be performed eventually but not under contract

5. Financial Statements
___Balance sheets for three to five years*
___P&L Statements for three to five years*
___Tax returns for three to five years

6. Credit
___Credit history of the business
___Amount of credit available from suppliers and vendors
___Terms of credit available from suppliers and other vendors

Control

1. Ownership Structure
___Form of ownership*
___Articles of incorporation; partnership and/or shareholder agreement
___Name of principals with more than 25 percent ownership*
___Name of minority shareholders
___List of shareholders not employed by the business
___Organization chart
___Fictitious name registrations

2. Strategic Alliances
___Vendor relationships
___Franchise agreements*
___Marketing and advertising agencies
___Accounting firms
___Law firms
___Commitments of time and money vs. services rendered from above
___Company attorney
___Insurance agent

3. Employee Relationships
___Employment contracts

___Agreements with independent contractors
___Independent contractors
___Employee manual
___Job descriptions
___Estimate of employee turnover rate and cost (ETOR and ETOC)*
___Procedure to locate, assess and hire employees
___Enforceable covenants not to compete
___Employee training programs

4. Location
___Property survey
___Zoning classification and restrictions
___Easements on the property
___Real estate taxes
___Property appraisal*
___Buildings and improvements*
___Floor plan of buildings and location of improvements

5. Administrative
___Licenses
___Insurance plans and policies
___Pending litigation*
___Contingent liabilities*
___Internet or Intranet-enabled administration procedures and protocols

Marketing

1. Business Mission Statement

2. Marketing Position

3. Marketing and Communication Strategy
___Advertising and marketing themes and appeals*
___Venues for spreading the marketing message
___Advertising contracts

___Agreements with advertising or marketing firms or agents

___Samples of marketing and advertising materials

___Marketing research to support position and strategy*

4. E-commerce Applications

___Web site address*

___# of hits per day

___Conversion rate of hits to sales*

___Linkages to other web site providers

___Describe business-to-business activity

5. Competitive Marketing Analysis

___Description of nearest competitor

___Number or competitors in trade area

___Market share*

___Marketing opportunities to expand current sales results

6. Growth Wall Analysis*

A growth wall is a condition that prevents progress and results. It stops a business dead in its tracks. The most obvious symptom is the end of a strong favorable trend of trailing revenue. It occurs because the environment around a business has changed but the business has not. For example, selling bell-bottom jeans was a big business in the 1960's. Companies still attempting to sell bell-bottom jeans today would likely fail. The market has changed. Thus, a growth wall presents considerable increase in business risk.

Professor Richard Osborne, Case Western Reserve University, describes the phase two (after the start-up has already passed) growth wall as common in the evolution of owner managed entrepreneurial companies. He notes several patterns inherent in companies that fail to penetrate a growth wall, including 1) sudden reversals in revenue after steady annual business increases; 2) diminished entrepreneurial energy; 3) gen-

*eralized internal focus; 4) falling behind the industry
trend change curve; 5) reactive product or service
development, distribution, and marketing; and 6)
absence of internal attitudes and competencies necessary to see and understand external threats.*

*To break through a growth wall, company managers
must reestablish the link between their product and
their market – the latter has changed and the former
has not. Business managers should study the environment in which the business operates to identify and recommend complimentary changes. The entrepreneur
who can recognize a growth wall in a business, and has
the ability to scale it may enjoy highly lucrative business
investment opportunities.*

Sales

1. Sales Results*
___Sales data*
___Annual trends
___Seasonal trends
___Time to create one sale
___Average sales price
___Average gross profit per sale
___Average net profit per sale
___Impact of sales cycles on cash flow*
___Record of cash flows by month*
___Record of deficit spending to sustain low sales
months

2. Description of Product or Service
___Transactional products
___Consulting services
___Enterprise relationships
___Key benefit to customer*

3. Sales Channels
___How are sales leads generated*

___How are sales made*
___Sales persons
___Telemarketing
___Direct mail
___Internet
___Other

4. Sales Management
___Sales lines of authority
___Sales person or employee span of control*
   ___Number of accounts one can handle
   ___Amount of sales floor one can handle
___Sales compensation formula*
___Base compensation
___Commission income
___Territorial assignments
___Geographically based
___Product based
___Treatment of reimbursable expenses
___Description of sales training

Production

1. Production
___Capacity to produce under existing conditions
___Limitations on capacity
___Variance between existing capacity and demand*
___Cost to increase capacity

2. List of Property
___Equipment
___Furnishings
___Fixtures
___Description of each of above
___Age and condition of equipment
___Obsolescence noted*
___Deferred maintenance noted*

3. Inventory
___Amount on hand to meet existing demand*
___End of year (EOY) changes in quantity of inventory on hand
___Inventory turnover ratio*
___Annual cost of goods / inventory at cost
___Accounting system to identify inventory on hand and needed
___Variance of inventory in peak versus low selling seasons
___Source of inventory and timing of delivery

4. Schematic of Work Flow
___Receipt of inventory
___Storage of inventory
___Description of production process if any*

Service

1. Services
___Services performed*
___Pricing structure for services
___Turnaround time for service work
___Who performs services to clients

2. Policies
___Product or service guarantees
___Returns & refunds*
___Payment
___Tracking system
___Managing complaints
___Annual cost of returns

3. Distribution of Service
___Where service is performed
___Profitability of service
___How products are returned
___Who pays cost of shipping

4. Training*
   ___Staff training of new personnel
   ___Employee education and seminars
   ___Outsourced service department

5. Intellectual Capital
   ___Unique sources*
   ___Key people
   ___Patents & copyrights
   ___Production processes
   ___Competitive intelligence
   ___Customer relationships*
   ___Institutionalized or related to key people
   ___Transferability of intellectual capital
   ___Control over intellectual capital
      ___Vested rights
      ___Non-disclosure agreements with key personnel

Chapter 3
Comprehending the Financial Statements

Discoveries collected must be assimilated and reconstructed prior to a business valuation estimate, because the latter is only as good as the data. By themselves, valuation formulas are inert calculations that don't change. Conscientious effort at this stage pays off with estimates that are more reliable and accurate.

As the analyst moves beyond discovery, selected information stands out. Some kinds are expressed numerically, others are not. The objective of a business valuation is to convert material that is subjective or qualitative into quantitative variables. This makes it possible to measure the relative value of a business in mathematical terms that are universally understood and accepted. A business is not priced high because it feels good – financial results justify the value.

Business Balance Sheet

Selected information about a business becomes an important database of variables used to energize the valuation formulas and produce a meaningful result. Some variables are less complicated to construct or have a singular use. They come from several sources. This chapter will focus on those contained in the business financial statements.

There are many names for a summary of a business's record of financial performance: "Books," "Profit and Loss Report," "Operating Statement," "EOY (End-of-Year) Results," "P & L" and "Income Summary" are a few. In general, they offer a description of the business results for the current and previous years.

A financial statement describes the business capital structure numerically. The financial statement has two basic parts: the balance sheet, which includes a list of business assets and liabilities (essence of the capital structure) and the operating statement, which is a record of business revenue, expenses and earnings.

Study the books or (financial framework) carefully. Hal Geneen, a modern-day business legend and author of *Managing* emphasizes this point best. "In business, numbers are the symbols by which you measure the various activities of an individual enterprise. They are not the business; they are only pictures of the business. Numbers serve as a sort of thermometer which measures the health and well-being of the enterprise." Penetrating the persona of a business through its numbers improves understanding of business capacity, problems and potential. Do not hurry when reviewing financial records. Time spent in this regard could be worth thousands of dollars per hour.

Assets

The first variables to know describe the value of assets included in a business. There are two measures to identify: book value of assets is the first, market value is the second. Both are affected, increased or decreased, by several factors.

A list of assets appears in the first or top section of the balance sheet. Assets are divided into two categories. These are current assets, including such things as cash-on-hand, accounts receivables, prepaid expenses, certain types of equipment and inventory. The second category includes larger items such as land and buildings, which are considered fixed assets.

The value assigned to each asset listed is taken from its original cost when placed in service. Also listed is an entry called "accumulated depreciation." This is a deduction representing a loss of asset value resulting from normal wear-and-tear in use. The amount of depreciation taken is subtracted from the asset's original cost. Asset values and accumulated depreciation are often grouped together for simplicity. The difference between original cost of assets and depreciation subtracted is the "book" value of business assets – their value as they appear in the business books.

Tangible vs. Intangible Assets. Frequently assets listed in a financial statement are only tangible – property one can touch and feel. Typically intangible assets are not included in the asset variable used to value the business. They differ because they cannot be touched or directly felt. Likewise, banks do not accept intangible assets as collateral for financing. Exceptions may occur, however, when intangible assets are directly connected to revenue creation. Patents, copyrights, secret formulas or production processes are common examples. These can be listed in the balance sheet summary of assets. The final estimate of asset value will be used in the excess earnings and leveraged cash flow valuation formulas presented in Chapter 6, 7 and 8.

Goodwill. In some cases goodwill is listed as an intangible asset. Confusion may surround the meaning of "goodwill" when the term is used to represent value in a business. In many cases an investor, acting on advice of a professional representative, will refuse to pay for goodwill as a part of the business price. The implication is goodwill is intangible, therefore, conveying nothing of value and not a fair exchange for cash or notes. The real intent, though, may be to avoid allocating any portion of the purchase price to goodwill. This is because goodwill according to IRC 197 is amortized on a straight-line basis over a 15-year period. It offers limited tax benefits compared to other assets with shorter depreciation or amortization periods.

One does not value goodwill separately from the business, or with no business value. These are valued together then separated. For income tax preparation, goodwill is the excess of purchase price for a business over the market value of all tangible assets. This is based on the "residual method" as prescribed in IRC 1060. This definition is consistent with the definition used in business valuation. There are cases when purchasing goodwill can be an attractive investment option, too.

Where goodwill is justifiable, it is not difficult to illustrate its value. Compare the cost to buy the benefits of goodwill (revenue, earnings, reputation, location, market position, procedures and product/service mix) with the investment required to build it (and the accompanying benefits) from scratch. Also, consider the time it takes to buy versus build. Keep in mind, the risk to a start-up business is often much greater than the risk of failure in a business already performing successfully. Sometimes buying goodwill is a good deal.

Obsolescence. This term indicates an asset, service or product is becoming obsolete and losing its value. It is important to recognize obsolescence because it will affect, favorably or unfavorably, the value of business assets. Old inventory not suitable for resale, for example, or equipment no longer in use might be discounted (perhaps below book value) when attempting to estimate tangible business asset values. Two kinds of obsolescence are important for the entrepreneur to consider.

Functional obsolescence occurs when the need or demand for an asset ceases to exist. For example, printing presses will become obsolete as demand for documents transmitted via the Internet grows. Already entire magazines are published electronically. This eliminates the cost of paper, printing and shipping, offering publishers a significant savings of manpower, time and money. The increased speed of production shortens the information cycle so the product timeliness and desirability improves, too. Books published directly on the Internet will contribute further to the growing obsolescence of printing presses.

Economic obsolescence, a second way assets become outdated, often occurs in tandem with its functional counterpart. Declining demand for "486" microprocessors was related to new software that would only run on Pentium microprocessors (functional obsolescence). Sales, and the economic value of the 486 chips and related software, were virtually erased. Economic obsolescence may also occur independently, however. A good example may be found in the business's heating and cooling system (HVAC). Significant improvements of energy efficiencies in HVAC equipment have occurred. Compared to old systems, new units do a better job managing air in the workplace environment. They also create savings, permitting their cost to be recovered in a few years. As a result, many business owners discover that, while still functional, old systems are too expensive to operate. Economic obsolescence has occurred and the value of the affected equipment is reduced.

In other instances, a lack of obsolescence may cause an asset's value to exceed its book value. Simple marketplace appreciation is a common reason. A building might have appreciated in value because of market trends even though it is being depreciated for tax purposes. Real estate values in good locations usually rise. Thus, original cost and book values are lower than the price investors would pay to acquire such a resource. In the alternative, an accelerated depreciation schedule may outpace the useful life of an asset to create a similar disparity between book and economic value.

This alone may occur when an asset value can be increased due to a unique/specific function – its highest and best use. For example, mobile home communities often purchase and rent used mobile homes. These are aggressively depreciated but can remain useful for many years. Suppose the rent collectable is $350 per month. Using the IRV business valuation formula and a 50% rate of return, the economic value of a single mobile home rental might be $8,400. The book value, however, could be zero.

Because the book value of each asset can be affected by functional or economic obsolescence, making appropriate adjustments in asset values improves accuracy of the business valuation estimate.

Market & Replacement Value. Market value is the amount one could reasonably expect to pay for an asset. It may be synonymous with replacement value or the cost to replace an asset with another of like kind. Neither reflects a property's book value nor its original cost – they are usually between. It may be difficult to develop a value estimate in which all can agree. To adjust, use original cost, book value, appraisals if available and discussions with ownership or knowledgeable industry professionals to develop a reasonable estimate of market or replacement asset values. More cooks will not spoil the stew.

When all is said and done, lenders tend to rely on book value as the basis for conservative loan approvals. Sellers want to use original or current economic value to raise the business price. Buyers try to use economic value to borrow and book value to buy. The analyst's job is to develop a complete the set of defensible key variables including book and market and replacement asset values. It will be used in the valuation formulas.

Liabilities

Following the list of assets on a balance sheet is a list of the business's debts, or liabilities. These are categorized as current or long-term. The former includes obligations such as accounts payable, operating lines of credit due within 90 days, accrued vacation pay, and so on. The latter typically includes loans secured to purchase the business, related property and equipment, or major capital improvements. Sometimes loans to shareholders will appear in this section. The current and long-term liabilities are combined to indicate the total liabilities of a business.

Equity

Subtracting existing debt from the net value of capital and property (and in some cases including intellectual capital) contributed to an investment yields the equity amount. Ownership equity in an acquisition is usually the down payment used to acquire a business. This is called "hard" equity because it represents a commitment of physical resources (e.g., cash). This does not always occur in a business acquisition, however. Some businesses are purchased wholly with borrowed funds, so there is no equity.

How then can equity be created where there is no original investment? Four forces combine to produce equity: income, tax benefits, amortization and appreciation.

Income. Without spending a dime for equity, it is possible to get a job and make a living wage. Ownership of a business should offer this, too, or the investment is questionable.

Tax Benefits. Businesses have the potential to offer tax savings on earnings compared with the same earnings provided by a job. Some businesses have deductions that reduce the earnings they create. The effect is to reduce taxable earnings and tax liability but not necessarily cash flow. Consequently, employment and business earnings could be the same, but the latter might be taxed at a lower marginal rate. A tax savings is the result.

Amortization. Business ownership can be like a savings account. If leveraged with reasonable financing and effective management, payment on debt comes from business earnings. A portion of payments is credited to interest on the outstanding loan: the remainder retires the principal until the debt is fully paid. Each principal payment represents a reduction in debt and, provided the business has not declined in value, a corresponding increase in ownership equity.

Appreciation. When a business appreciates, its value grows. Business revenue and earnings increase because of effective management, favorable market forces and a variety of other reasons. Normally increases in earnings are translated into greater business value, and the increase becomes added equity for ownership.

The combination of income, tax benefits, amortization and appreciation have an effect on ownership equity similar to compounding. Many underestimate the total effect magnified by an improved ability to buy low and sell high.

In additional to hard equity, there is another type called "sweat equity" – created by entrepreneurs with the management skill to run a business successfully. If the business grows in value, additional equity is the result. Management entrepreneurs can receive stock or ownership in lieu of a portion of their salary or in the place of bonuses. This is normal and accompanied by performance measurements to ensure stock is not given freely. Unlike hard equity, this form comes from an investment of time, focus and energy. It provides a convenient way for entrepreneurs to acquire a business interest with nothing down.

The amount of equity in a business can affect its value. Businesses with little or no debt are sometimes perceived as more stable and secure. Absence of debt suggests a business that can withstand changes in sales cycles, capitalize on unexpected market opportunities, compensate employees well and show little or no deferred maintenance or obsolescence in furnishings and equipment. This perception of security may generate a premium value compared to businesses burdened by heavy debt – provided the absence of debt is not accompanied by a sense of complacency on the part of management.

Sometimes a section of the balance sheet shows a reconciliation of *stockholder* or *owner's equity*. This is not the same as the business's value. It is also not a measurement of equity based on the business value estimate, but instead, is benchmarked against the book value. (Business book value is the book value of all assets minus liabilities.)

Generally owner's equity is a function of cash paid for the business or stock in the company, additional cash paid into the company and earnings that have been allowed to remain in the business (called *retained earnings*). The owner's equity portion of the balance sheet also describes the amount of stock the company is authorized to issue the *par* (nominal or face) value of each share and the number of share outstanding.

Balance Sheet
XYZ Company

Assets

CURRENT ASSETS

Inventory at Cost		$ 55,000.00
Accounts Receivable		$ 13,498.41
Prepaid Expenses		$ 2,401.08
Security Deposits		$ 675.00
Cash in Accounts		$ 19,904.66
Furnishings and Equipment		$ 15,000.00
Accumulated Depreciation	<$ 15,000.00>	
Net Current Assets		$ 91,479.15

FIXED ASSETS

Land @ Cost		$ 7,500.00
Building		$ 80,000.00
Accumulated Depreciation	<$ 29,333.00>	
Net Building		$ 50,667.00
Intangibles and Goodwill		$ 25,000.00
Accumulated Amortization	<$ 18,333.00>	
Net Intangibles and Goodwill		$ 6,667.00
Net Fixed Assets		$ 64,834.00

TOTAL ASSETS $156,313.15

Liabilities

CURRENT LIABILITIES

Accounts Payable	$ 33,127.50
Expenses Due	$ 7,638.00
Operating Credit Line	0.00
Employee Benefits/ Taxes Payable	$ 542.88
Total Current Liabilities	$ 41,308.38

LONG TERM LIABILITIES

Bank Loan on Business	$ 49,323.13

TOTAL LIABILTIES $ 90,631.51

OWNERSHIP EQUITY $ 65,681.64

TOTAL LIABILITIES AND EQUITY $156,313.15

Profit & Loss Statement

The second part of the financial statement describes business revenue, expenses and profit or loss created from operations. This document provides the most important data needed to develop a coherent business value.

The analyst should copy data from this section of the financial statement onto a standardized Profit & Loss Statement. (One can be easily created using the example at the end of this section.) This is a detailed but valuable exercise. When copying data the entrepreneur's attention is directed to each entry. Besides speeding up familiarity with the business it will also prompt important questions for management to consider, such as "How was [an expense] created?" or "Why is [an item] increasing or decreasing?" and "Is [a certain expense] necessary to operate the business?" Asking such questions prior to an earnings reconstruction (see Chapter Four) frequently unearths new data to offer a clearer picture of the business earning power.

Placing financial data into a familiar format has other benefits, too. Familiarity reduces difficulty. This is important since business financial statements are constructed in a variety of formats. Using the same format with each new analysis makes the job easier. In addition, forms presented in this text highlight key data linked to valuation formulas that follow. When transferring data to the analyst's forms certain items will appear that are common to most businesses. A discussion of them follows.

Revenue

Revenue is created by a business's sales or services. Gross income does not include revenue from sources unrelated to the principal business activity (e.g., interest on bank deposits owned by the business, earnings or rents from investments made and owned by the business, etc.). Observe the trend of revenue during previous years, taking note of significant increases or decreases. Attempt to correlate trends with specific events related to management or the marketplace – therein lies the reason they may have occurred, which provides valuable insight into business planning.

Cost of Goods

"Cost of goods" represents the total wholesale, cost of merchandise purchased or produced for resale. In retail, distributing or wholesaling business items purchased are sold at a higher price. In a restaurant, cost of goods is often referred to as "food cost" or the cost of bulk food purchased to produce the meals served. Manufacturing businesses include the cost of raw materials and labor required to build the finished product in their cost of goods calculations.

Calculate cost of goods by subtracting the cost of all merchandise purchased during the year from revenue. Take a second step and examine cost of goods as a percent of revenue; this can be revealing. In times of increasing business activity, cost of goods as a percent of revenue might remain fixed or decrease slightly. Increases in the percent of cost of goods may accompany declining revenues. Inventory taken for owners' use is another reason cost of goods could increase. Anticipation of a business sale is a third reason. Poor cash flows that restrict the ability to maintain inventory at optimum levels also accompany falling revenues.

Gross Profit

Gross profit is revenue less cost of goods. When calculating a product's retail price from its wholesale cost, the percent of markup is added to the wholesale price. Suppose an item costs $10.00 and the markup for resale is 50%. One would take 50% of $10.00 ($5.00) and add it to the cost of the product ($10.00) resulting in a sales price of $15.00. But notice, even though the markup is 50%, the gross margin (gross profit when stated as a percent of the retail price instead of wholesale cost) is 33%. The latter percentage is calculated by dividing the resale price into the amount of markup ($5÷$15). It is important to differentiate between markup and margin in conversation. Here's why:

Occasionally it is necessary to quickly size up a business without the benefit of financial records. This occurs when a broker is attempting to list a business or when an entrepreneur is casually investigating a business he or she may want to buy. Even though the books are not available, many sellers are still willing to have a casual conversation. A little information can be very revealing for those who adopt a more ingenious approach.

A first impression of business profitability can be created from three simple, non-threatening questions.

- *What is the average revenue per month?*
- *What is the average markup on merchandise or services?*
- *What are the average operating costs per month?*

Divide the average monthly revenue by 1.00 + the percent of markup on merchandise sold. The answer is the cost of goods per month. Subtract this amount from revenue to determine gross profit. Subtract monthly expenses from gross profit. The answer is an estimate of business cash flow.

For example, sales are $50,000 per month and merchandise is marked up an average of 30%. Cost of goods = $50,000÷130% = $38,461.54. Gross profit is $50,000 - $38,461.54 = $11,538.46. Estimated cash expenses to run the business are $6,000 per month. Estimated cash flow is $11,538.46 - $6,000, or $5,538.46 per month. Annual cash flow is $66,461.53.

Now the entrepreneur can determine if the business's earning power justifies continued interest. If so, the due diligence that follows will attempt to first confirm these initial conclusions.

In another situation, understanding ways to calculate gross revenue from cost of goods, and the inverse, is helpful. This is in taking a business inventory prior to the sale of a company. It is necessary to determine how much inventory is present and included in the sale price. The physical inventory is typically taken by an outside inventory service that counts all the merchandise based on retail price. This method is faster than checking thousands of items against their original invoiced cost.

Suppose, for the sell-out exercise, inventory is marked up 30% and has a retail value of $75,000. By subtracting 30% from $75,000, the indicated wholesale value could be $52,500. This, however, is an incorrect approach to the valuation of the inventory. Thirty percent of the expected resale price is more than 30% of the actual cost. The actual wholesale value is $57,692, or $5,192 more. This is because the retail value is 130% of the cost of goods. Therefore, when the retail value ($75,000) is divided by 130%, the actual wholesale value of the inventory is $57,692.31.

Operating Expenses

All the costs of running a business are the business expenses. They include insurance, payroll, depreciation, interest, maintenance, rent, office supplies, freight, automobile and travel expenses, and so forth. Keep two things in mind when reviewing a business's record of expenses.

While frugality is an important management virtue, it is possible to take this strategy too far. As Thomas E. Woods, former CFO of Trans World Airlines, has said, *"You cannot save yourself into prosperity."* Cost cutting, taken to the extreme, translates into declining business potential and, thereafter, loss of the business's capacity to serve demands from existing revenue. Here begins a vicious cycle. Expense reductions are not too difficult to make. They will, however, increase the workload and stress on existing employees and resources needed to fill the gap created. If not restored to previous levels, production and service may decline. Sales will likely decrease. This causes more expense reductions, which is the cycle renewing itself in a business that is slowly bleeding to death.

A classic example of this scenario occurs when the budget axe hits marketing and advertising budgets in response to poor revenue performance. Revenue and brand awareness go hand in hand. Indeed, in these days of electronic commerce the "brand" floating in cyberspace is often all the customer knows. So market awareness and revenue have become inseparable. It is good to remember that cutting expenses is a short-term fix and a finite strategy to improve profitability. Keeping the focus on ways to increase revenue has infinite possibilities and, though painful in the short term, can insure long-term prosperity.

The second characteristic of expenses is business owners intentionally maximize them to minimize earnings and tax liability. Therefore, a thorough review of expenses is a valuable prerequisite to the completion of an earnings reconstruction. It turns out expenses, not skimming, are the source of cash flow not indicated in business EBIT.

Earnings

Subtracting expenses from gross profit calculates earnings, known as "business net profit," "net operating income," "NOI," "profit," "taxable income," "EBIT (earnings before income taxes)" and so on. Typically earnings are stated after depreciation, amortization and interest as well as all other expenses are deducted. EBIT is the most commonly used and fundamental indicator of business performance.

In conversation with others, it is important to define precisely what type of earnings are being discussed. Sometimes mass confusion reigns. Frequently, the meaning of earnings varies from entrepreneur to entrepreneur. Variances in the definition of earnings – entrepreneur to seller or buyer or broker – can produce catastrophic results. When allowed to continue, such misunderstandings can hinder the valuation process and negatively affect its intended use thereafter.

Earnings Summary. An earnings summary is an abbreviated version of the business operating statement. It will include the basic key variables just mentioned: gross revenue, cost of goods, gross profit, expenses and earnings.

EARNINGS SUMMARY

Revenue	$608,951.00
Cost of Goods	<$397,530.00>
Gross Profit	$211,421.00
Expenses	<$190,501.29>
Earnings	$ 20,919.71

These, or variants of each, appear in most business operating statements. The earnings summary helps simplify the problem of becoming acquainted quickly with a business operating statement. Look for the earnings summary to simplify the investigation.

Trailing Earnings. Trailing earnings are earnings recorded during previous years of business operation. These are important to consider because they represent the rock-hard reality of a business's performance – not its potential. Valuations are more often based on the former and not the latter. Remember, history remains the best predictor of future performance.

Examining trailing earnings is also important because businesses are in a constant state of change. Creating business value from one year of performance does not take into consideration business trends. These could be highly favorable or unfavorable, thereby affecting business value; so, effective valuations use trailing earnings as a way to introduce the influence of trends into estimates of business value. For the sophisticated entrepreneur, trailing earnings trends provide the basis for forecasting future earnings. For most, however, trailing earnings are useful to weight cash flows that already exist and influence variables used in creating a risk/price multiple, described in the next chapter.

XYZ Company Business Profit & Loss Statement
January 1 through December 31

REVENUE

Gross Sales		$581,282.00
Service Income		$ 27,669.00
Total Revenue		$608,951.00

COST OF GOODS

Merchandise Purchases	$376,778.25	
Labor on Service	$ 20,751.75	
Total Cost of Goods		<$397,530.00>

GROSS PROFIT $211,421.00

OPERATING EXPENSES

Advertising	$ 36,913.50	
Amortization	$ 1,667.66	
Auto & Truck	$ 332.00	
Commissions	$ 6,187.12	
Depreciation	$ 4,809.00	
Dues & Subscriptions	$ 179.00	
Entertainment	$ 1,776.00	
Equipment Lease	$ ——	
Freight	$ 11,378.60	
Insurance	$ 2,835.00	
Interest	$ 4,533.29	
Janitorial	$ 3,882.00	
Laundry & Uniforms	$ 900.00	
Licenses	$ 75.00	
Non-Recurring Expenses	$ 501.66	
Payroll	$ 61,871.22	
Payroll Taxes	$ 4,604.34	
Professional Fees	$ 900.00	
Real Estate Taxes	$ 5,743.00	
Rent	$ ——	
Repairs & Maintenance	$ 2,700.00	
Salaries (Owner's)	$ 18,000.00	
Sales Taxes	$ ——	
Supplies Office	$ 421.00	
Travel	$ 1,487.53	
Telephone	$ 2,964.00	
Utilities	$ 12,828.00	
Other	$ 3,012.37	
Total Expenses	$190,501.29	

Earnings Before Income Taxes (EBIT) $ 20,919.71

Chapter 4
Reconstructing Business Earnings

Entrepreneurs build certain variables using basic data collected in a due diligence. These are more meaningful and will be used in valuation formulas. Note, they are not particularly difficult to develop, but maintaining accuracy is very important. For example, cash flow is the base variable from which the valuation estimate is built. If it is incorrect, valuation estimates can be equally off the mark. Take great care when building these indicators of value. Like levers, a small change may correctly or incorrectly magnify the outcome.

EBIT and Cash Flow

Recall obsolescence affects the value of business assets. Depending on the particular situation, an asset could be worth more or less than its book value. The entrepreneur conducting a business valuation needs to adjust asset values to account for obsolescence that may have occurred. An earnings reconstruction (ERCON) does the same to resolve a discrepancy between apparent and actual earnings.

The ERCON is performed after the analyst has become familiar with the business's financial statements. With the ERCON, key variables may be developed: EBITDA, cash flow and weighted cash flow. The latter is used in the capitalization, excess earnings and leveraged cash flow methods of business valuation.

An ERCON is necessary because business owners frequently maximize expenses to minimize earnings. This is a strategy of tax avoidance used to limit taxable earnings so tax liability may be reduced. It is also a catch-22. To the untrained or inexperienced, the EBIT figure does not seem appealing and makes a business investment less attractive. This situation is the real reason most owners resist financial disclosures to potential buyers of their business.

Simply put, business EBIT will seldom justify a price constructed using the business cash flow or free cash flow. An owner knows the difference between what is reported for tax purposes and what he or she actually gets to keep. Explaining it to a buyer is a challenge. But when access to financial details of a business is denied, an ERCON and subsequent valuations cannot be completed. So, ownership's tax avoidance strategy becomes an albatross around their neck. It can prevent them from adequate justifications of value. This is a broker's opportunity. Resolving the issue enables parties involved to see clearly how a selected value is justified. EBITDA is a popular example of the simplest type of ERCON and is regularly used by many business professionals.

EBITDA

EBITDA is another form of business cash flow. It is EBIT plus two expenses that are often treated as additional cash flow to the business. The letters "D" and "A" stand for *depreciation* and *amortization*, which are typically listed as expenses. But ownership does not pay any cash for these items. They are deductions. The acronym therefore represents Earnings Before Income Taxes, Depreciation & Amortization.

The IRS takes the position that investments in tangible and certain intangible assets (see Chapter 3) may be recovered over time by the taxpayer. The vehicle used to accomplish this is a prorated share of their original value charged as an expense to the business operation. This is a substitute for treating the original cost as an expense in the first year the asset was acquired. Consequently, since the original cost was paid in the beginning, the amount expensed each year does not represent cash paid out. It is, therefore, a deduction only and may be added back to EBIT. The resulting macro variable, EBITDA, is often considered a more accurate reflection of business earnings available to ownership.

Depreciation. Certain assets used in the production of business income can be deducted from gross revenue either directly or indirectly. This is how the Internal Revenue Service enables business owners to recover the cost of assets purchased by the business, hence the alternative name – "cost recovery." Depreciation expenses are added to earnings to complete one-half of the acronym: EBITD.

There are three cost recovery or depreciation systems in place. These were created by the Economic Recovery Tax Act of 1981 (ERTA) and revised by the Tax Reform Act of 1986. The system taxpayers use depends on when the property depreciated was placed in service. Methods of depreciation based on rules of financial accounting are contained in IRC (Internal Revenue Code) 167: the Accelerated Cost Recovery System (ACRS) and the Modified Accelerated Cost Recovery System (MACRS). These mandate the portion of an asset that can be deducted each year. To simplify, the systems are straight-line (equal amount each year) or variable.

Direct deductions include cost of goods and other perishables such as office supplies. Indirect deductions occur when the asset's useful life extends beyond a typical business period (one year). In these cases a portion of the asset's value is deducted each year to represent the eventual wasting of the asset that occurs. When fully depreciated an asset's book value can be zero.

Some assets cannot be depreciated. Personal assets, a home or a car not used for business are examples. Other assets with an indefinite life, such as land, are not depreciated either.

Amortization. Amortization is the depreciation of intangible assets. It appears as a deduction in the expense section of a business operating statement. Unlike their tangible counterparts, intangible assets are amortized on a straight-line basis. The typical amortization period is 15 years.

IRC 197 indicates amortization applies to assets acquired by the business that are actively used to produce income. It does not indicate intangibles created by the business can be amortized. However, in certain cases assets such as copyrights and patents that have been shown to have definite limited lives may be amortized.

Examples of intangible assets that can be amortized are goodwill and other intangibles purchased; start-up costs; organization costs; research and experimental costs; a covenant not to compete; patents; copyrights; and customer lists. Amortization expenses are added to business earnings to complete the variable: EBITDA. This is a more accurate indicator of the business earning power. A sample EBITDA calculation follows:

CALCULATING EBITDA	
Revenue	$608,951
Cost of Goods	<$397,530>
Gross Profit	$211,421
Expenses	<$190,501>
EBIT (Earnings)	$ 20,920
Depreciation	$ 4,809
Amortization	$ 1,668
EBITDA	$ 27,397

Cash Flow

Although depreciation and amortization are two widely accepted additions to business earnings, there are others. These can be related to the purpose of a valuation that may include a significant change in management strategy or sale of the business. The analyst will attempt to see past the transition planned and identify new expenses that do not exist under the present circumstances. Expenses could create increases or decreases in EBITDA. These adjustments, positive and negative, are added or subtracted from EBITDA to identify a business's "cash flow." Used in this more common vernacular, cash flow is very often greater. It is earnings available to ownership following the expected change in business strategy or ownership, provided the previous year's business results remain unchanged. Cash flow therefore is a critical variable.

Weighted Cash Flow

There are occasions when use of one year's cash flow increases investment risk. A weighted cash flow is helpful when a business is experiencing strong growth trends or downturns in results. This device will diminish the influence of trends on business cash flow and is used as a replacement for one year's cash flow. This approach is less aggressive but it remains reliable thereby reducing risk to the investor.

To calculate a weighted cash flow, the current year and the previous one or two years of operating statements are used. An ERCON is performed with each year. Thereafter, a weighting scale is used. When using the current and one previous year, the current year cash flow is multiplied by 2 and added to the previous year. The result is then divided by 3. Thus the final cash flow estimate used is weighted two-to-one in favor of the current year.

When three years of results are used, the current year is multiplied by 3, the previous year by 2, and the earliest year is added. The combined result is divided by 6, and the cash flow bears a 3:2:1 weighting. Again, current trends are given greater emphasis but not used exclusively for the valuation analysis.

The objective of an ERCON is to clearly identify expenses that might be adjusted. Many times the process is improved by conversations with ownership. Ease into this conversation by first explaining the purpose for the investigation into business expenses. Describe the benefit of discovering the business's true earning power. A good question to make this case is "Which indicator of performance can justify a higher value-taxable earnings or cash flow?" Explained this way, owners understand the value of disclosures. In fact, some tell more than they should.

"Perks": Positive Adjustments to Earnings

There are several types of expenses that may be added in part or entirely to earnings. Many will fall into the following categories: education, employee benefits, entertainment, home office, interest, non-recurring expenses, payroll, transportation and travel in addition to depreciation and amortization. The discussion that follows includes references to the deductibility of certain expenses according to the current Internal Revenue

Service Code. Taxation rules and regulations are sometimes warped beyond recognition by ownership pursuing an aggressive tax avoidance strategy. The general effect of this distortion of justification for certain expenses provides the basis for adjustment-addition to earnings. Conference with professional representatives of the business to help determine when and if such instances occur.

Education

Education expenses can be deducted provided the purpose of the education is deemed required or necessary for the pursuit of business activity. Generally, if the education is needed to improve business skills or meet legal or licensing requirements, it is deductible.

It is fairly easy to imagine a situation where a buyer is acquiring a business with considerable experience. Education expenses for employees of or the previous owner may no longer be necessary; thus, these could be considered additions to earnings.

Employee Benefits

Employee benefits are paid to employees of the business who receive compensation. The most common form of employee benefit is insurance. Medical insurance is costly, and premiums paid to a departing owner may be considered cash flow if not reassigned to a new owner. The same can be said of life insurance used to fund an estate, or company contributions to a pension plan. If not to be paid to new ownership, these are adjustments to earnings.

Entertainment

Entertaining clients in the course of business is a common practice (sometimes more necessary than desired). Ownership entertaining itself is not the same, however. Entertainment expenses are deductible according to IRC 162 or 212 if they are considered directly related or associated with business activity.

Abuses occur when the entertainment is less related to business and more related to personal enjoyment. As a result, strict rules to govern the deductibility of entertainment expenses appear in IRC 274. This section indicates 50% of entertainment and meal expenses are allowed for deductions provided they are not considered excessive. If it is suggested that entertainment expenses are greater than necessary, that portion not required may be added to earnings.

Home Office

The most rapidly growing form of business deductions emerging are those related to use of a home office. This is a result of the rapid expansion of telecommuting opportunities and the formation of home-based businesses. The Taxpayers Relief Act of 1997 (TRA 1997) provides that business deductions for home expenditures can be made if the office 1) Is used as a principal place of business for the business activity, 2) Is used as a location to meet clients or customers during the normal course of business, or 3) Is located in a structure not attached to the home but at the same location.

Deductions made are those that relate directly or indirectly to the office. This covers basic operating expenses, decorating and a prorated share of expenses that benefit the entire home. These would be mortgage interest or rent, real estate taxes, insurance, utilities and maintenance.

When a home-based business is to be acquired and moved, it is evident the home office business expenses will be discontinued. If the current owner makes deductions for the home office, they may be treated as adjustments to earnings. They will be discontinued under new ownership and cease to exist.

Interest

Mortgage interest costs are usually removed as a cost of doing business when performing an ERCON. This is because valuation formulas begin with cash flow as the primary driver of value. Committing 95% of a company's cash flow to the payment of a large mortgage may affect business equity. Value however is the combination of equity and debt. Since most valuations are performed to serve an acquisition objective, new financing is often contemplated. Therefore, interest costs related to existing financing on a business are often treated as positive adjustments to earnings.

An exception with interest can occur when financing is needed to support normal business operations. This frequently happens when inventory is financed and there is no plan to own this asset outright. Interest costs related to maintenance of an inventory would not be added to earnings provided there is no change of strategy to eliminate them altogether.

Another occasion will exist when the business has wide variances in selling cycles creating the need for large cash reserves. Unless operations are funded from ownership equity (cash), interest tied to a line of credit will occur. These are not added as adjustments to earnings.

Non-recurring Expenses

There may be instances when expenses have been incurred but will not be repeated. This occurs with expenses that may be expensed rather than depreciated or amortized over time. Typical examples of non-recurring expenses are certain types of repairs and maintenance, an increase in the business inventory, addition of small equipment and so forth. If it is recognized that these costs were unique and will occur only once, they may become adjustments to earnings.

Payroll

It is common for owners of a business to pay themselves a salary. This will normally be found in the salaries or general payroll expense. It may also be placed in the officers' salaries when the business is a corporation.

In general, payroll and officers' salaries may be considered adjustments to earnings when one of the following two conditions exists. First, payment is made from either expense to compensate a departing operating owner who can be adequately replaced by a new operating owner. They will acquire the existing owner's payroll and/or officer's salary. Second are payments to compensate individuals who do not perform services for the company. Sometimes this occurs with board members or a CEO advisory board. They are compensated from officers' salaries in exchange for their participation at quarterly board meetings. If deemed unnecessary by new ownership, this expense may be treated as an adjustment to earnings.

In some cases, only a portion of the compensation to an existing owner will be recaptured as earnings. One example occurs when a new owner feels the owner's existing compensation should be split between themselves and some other type of new expense – perhaps an additional employee. Another occasion arises when a new owner elects to commit a portion of the current owner's compensation to payment of financing created to acquire the business. (This is discussed in greater detail within subsequent chapters.)

On occasion a new owner will reduce the staff of a business. This can occur if existing management has been in place for many years, has become complacent or tends to favor certain employees despite their level of performance. Eliminating jobs or people is an unpleasant as well as risky management tactic for a new owner. On the surface it does not capture the trust or loyalty of remaining employees either. Cutbacks can, however, be very timely and appropriate, plus produce a desired result – improved earnings. When this is the case, firm, decisive management is rewarded with improved earnings. This will reestablish the confidence, pride and support needed from company employees.

Conversely, no adjustment to earnings occurs when new management does not plan to replace existing management and assume their wages. This occurs occasionally when entrepreneurs target a business for addition to their portfolio and encourage existing management to continue. Or, they may hire new management altogether. Wages paid to existing management are not earnings adjustments.

Transportation

Transportation costs deducted are taxi fares, train fares, airline tickets, and so forth. These are deductible when they occur in the course of travel for business purposes. Most common of the transportation expenses is the automobile and truck expense, which frequently appears in the business operating statement. Methods of determining the auto expense taken will vary. The bigger question pertains to the use of the vehicle for business or personal purposes. Answering this question will determine the availability of adjustment if warranted.

Travel

Generally speaking, travel expenses are deductible if the owner traveled to engage in trade or business activity. Travel expenses include transportation, meals, lodging and other reasonable and necessary expenses while "away from home." The IRS takes the position that to qualify, the person traveling must be away from home overnight or for a period of time that will require some rest before returning home. Many business owners will participate in business and personal activities when traveling. The question of deductibility often occurs. The prevailing determinant is whether the travel was business or personal. There are many other rules that govern the deductibility of travel expenses. These can be found in IRC 274. In any event, some travel costs appearing in business expenses may be personal or entirely unnecessary in the future. Therefore, a positive adjustment is calculated as the extent to travel costs are reduced. It is added to earnings.

The amount of adjusting estimated to occur is limited only by entrepreneurial creativity. These will always be found in the expenses of the business. Draws to ownership appearing in the balance sheet are not positive adjustments. Suspicious increases in cost of goods inferring owner's use of personal merchandise are not positive adjustments. Skimming is not. Nevertheless, when all are considered, these adjustments are capable of producing dramatic changes in the business earning power recognized. This will directly affect business value.

"Plows": Negative Adjustments to Earnings

Negative adjustments earn the nickname "Plows" because they dig into and reduce business EBIT. These are expenses the business does not have prior to a transition but will incur afterward. They are not particularly common, but it is always wise to try and detect their presence.

There are many examples of negative adjustments. The most obvious is an increase in leased payments or rent occurring as a condition of a business transfer. Recent property assessments may create a rise in business or real property taxes. The husband and wife team departing as operating owners may create a need for another employee. New marketing to expand business share could be necessary. Deferred maintenance or new equipment purchases for expansion are another.

To identify negative adjustments, discuss current operations with ownership. What improvements to the business are desirable-which are required? The latter, together with any other negative adjustments, should be subtracted from EBIT.

Cash Flow Calculation

The completed ERCON presents a very clear estimate of the business's earning power. As previously stated, this is the business cash flow. This number may be a derivative of the most current business operating statement, or a weighted average of the past three.

As an ERCON is performed, the buyer begins to see why a business can have many different values. Adjustments to earnings available to one investor may not be suitable for another. A situation involving any of those adjustments previously discussed could be found to apply. As a result, the cash flow available will bear a corresponding difference. The chapters explaining valuation techniques will illustrate how cash flow affects value, too. More cash flow tends to produce a higher value, and the reverse is also true.

EARNINGS RECONSTRUCTION

Revenue	$608,951
Cost of Goods	<$397,530>
Gross Profit	$211,421
Expenses	<$190,501>
EBIT (Earnings)	$ 20,920
Depreciation	$ 4,809
Amortization	$ 1,668
EBITDA	$ 27,397
Mortgage Interest	$ 4,533
Non-Recurring Expenses	$ 502
Owner's Salary	$ 18,000
Net Adjustments to EBITDA	$ 23,053
CASH FLOW	$ 50,432

Here, then, is a quantifiable explanation for the premise that one business could be worth more or less depending on the needs of the interested investor. Those who can extract the most adjustments and cash flow realize benefits that actually improve the value as offered. For this reason, mergers to achieve the benefits of consolidation have become a popular acquisition method. Earnings remain the same but adjustments to expenses can be maximized. Other investors unable to retrieve all adjustments available from a consolidation discover they must pay the price or pass.

In the end, the entrepreneur does not attempt to build a one-size-fits-all value estimate. The better approach is to define a value range. Where a business sale is anticipated, the reconstruction and value estimate is designed to meet the needs of most buyers in the largest target market. Setting the stage to attract the most investors available has the best chance of producing a successful result. The best value is the one the greatest number of investors in the target profile are willing to pay. Business valuation is a powerful marketing tool.

Ownership Versus Management: Compensation Issues

It is very common for one person to wear the hat of owner and manager in a small business. As a result they receive the dual benefits available to ownership and management. This can be a significant benefit of small business ownership. Attempting to wear both hats simultaneously, however, is a more challenging proposition. For example, both a cowboy hat and baseball cap shelter the sun from the wearer's eyes. They perform similar if not identical functions. But attempting to wear them both at the same time does not improve the result. In fact, the benefit of each, albeit slightly different, is reduced. Their only real compatibility is that they both fit the same head, but not necessarily at the same time.

The story about hats is an important metaphor to remember at this stage of business valuation. The reason is the cash flow of many small business operations may be insufficient to pay management compensation at "market rates" plus generate a handsome return to ownership. This does not, however, diminish interest in small business ownership for the purpose of creating an employment opportunity for oneself. Indeed, the same people that own them also manage most small businesses. They want to make an investment and experience the thrill and autonomy provided by entrepreneurship. The danger lies in attempting to fill the roles of ownership and management simultaneously. It takes focus to execute the responsibilities of both positions efficiently. Distractions, reducing focus, are the frequent result of acting both as manager and owner. This can lead to poor financial results – a primary cause of business failure.

Establishing a Pay Rate

The leveraged cash flow methods of business valuation will require management costs to be considered before a value is determined. Therefore, it is necessary to determine accurate management costs prior to calculating business value. As discussed this should be considered separately from return on ownership rewards to ownership, even though the owner and manager might be the same person.

Several approaches to assign management compensation are available to the valuation analyst. The current ownership compensation package is always a good example to consider. However, many times the employment earnings of owner/operators will have become inconsistent with the local market – they own the place and can pay themselves as much or as little as they like. In come cases the salary will be small and supplemented with business profits. In others the salary is large compared to compensation for similar jobs in other businesses. It is wise to be careful when using existing management compensation (to an operating owner) as a benchmark to estimate the future cost of business supervision.

An alternative way to determine management compensation involves going directly to the market. Research wages offered by other companies to those who would fill supervisory roles similar in skill requirements, responsibility and authority. Newspaper classifieds, industry trade journals, local accountants, lenders and competitors are good sources of accurate information. Analysts have been known to conduct surveys as a device to encourage participation and legitimate input. The results of the survey are distributed to contributors who receive the benefit of this valuable market information.

The U.S. Government provides a third source of data entrepreneurs can use to determine management compensation. One document available and of particular interest is called "Household Data Annual Averages." This material describes the results of a nationwide survey of compensation amounts for hundreds of employment positions. The data shows occupation, year of survey, number of workers included in the survey, and median weekly earnings for each worker. It also indicates earning variances between men and women.

The Household Data report provides a rich source of current information for the business valuation consultant. To use it correctly, identify one or more positions that match or are similar to the management position in the business under study. Working with one of these median weekly earnings values (or the average of several), multiply the weekly earnings by 52 (the number of weeks in the year) to estimate annual management costs. As simple as that. However, it is wise to challenge this estimate by comparing it to local pay levels. Thereafter, make any adjustments felt necessary in order to account for geographic or economic variances. The tables, appearing in the Appendix Section, are reprinted from the archives and current data on file with the United States Bureau of Labor Statistics.

For the example used in this text, it is assumed the business is a sales-oriented enterprise. From the job classification "Supervisors," in the Proprietors/Sales Occupations, the average median weekly income is $587. This is $30,524 per year and will be used to estimate business free cash flow.

Free Cash Flow

The rewards of ownership and employment (management) become as different as the contribution required to create them. Think of it: by providing capital and financing, an entrepreneur can own a business without operating it. Conversely, a manager can apply experience, skill and time to manage a business successfully but not own it. One is concerned directly with business value – the other indirectly. Therefore, to calculate business value the analyst must separate the costs of management from financial rewards of ownership, as explained previously. Then business value is a derivative of earning power, assuming all the pieces and parts to deliver the return on investment are firmly in place. Leaving anything out results in an overestimation of value. The remaining funds, representing the financial reward to ownership, are free cash flow. Like its compensation counterpart, this will be used extensively in the valuation estimates.

Calculating free cash flow is easy. Cash flow is determined by performing an ERCON. When completed, the cost of management compensation is subtracted from cash flow. Free cash flow is the remainder. Examine the formula to determine this variable:

FREE CASH FLOW CALCULATION	
Revenue	$608,951
Cost of Goods	<$397,530>
Gross Profit	$211,421
Expenses	<$190,501>
EBIT (Earnings)	$ 20,920
Depreciation	$ 4,809
Amortization	$ 1,668
EBITDA	$ 27,397
EBITDA	$ 27,397
Mortgage Interest	$ 4,533
Non-Recurring Expenses	$ 502
Owner's Salary	$ 18,000
Net Adjustments to EBITDA	$ 23,053
CASH FLOW	$ 50,432
Management Compensation	<$ 30,500>
FREE CASH FLOW	$ 19,932

Playing It Safe

As variables for valuation are developed, they become standards to define realistic investment expectations for management and ownership. Decisions of considerable size are made based on these interpretations of data. It is best to take a conservative approach, but what is conservative to one is very often not so safe to another.

For example, conservative to a buyer could mean selecting a capitalization rate that is very high thus driving the value down. Conservative to a seller, on the other hand, often means reducing management compensation to the bare minimum thereby increasing free cash flow. This has the effect of increasing business value. Taking a conservative approach, however, is not demonstrated by either of these tactics designed only to protect the interests of a specific client.

The truly conservative approach is neutral and derived from an objective interpretation of the data intrinsic and extrinsic to the business under review. It requires balancing the excitement of buying or selling against marketplace variables that can be backed up (to the extent possible) with facts. A value calculated in these conditions will often meet the needs of all parties to a transaction. Buyers will not go broke attempting to make a deal that simply costs too much: sellers will not languish in the market until it's time to give up and liquidate for half the original business value.

Therefore, the truly conservative approach is an aggressive valuation strategy that makes good economic sense – is destined to get results. A superior business value will instantly attract entrepreneurs who are ready, willing and able to buy. When one performs sellers can make an honorable exit with a legitimate settlement in hand in exchange for all he or she has built. And both can move forward to their next entrepreneurial adventure.

Chapter 5
Rules of Thumb for Business Financing

Buying a business may be the largest investment an entrepreneur will make. However, the amount of cash needed to buy a business "outright" is often more than most entrepreneurs have "on hand." Fortunately, it is possible to start small and grow. But financing makes it possible to start a little bigger and grow a little faster.

Once a business is acquired growing can require cash, too – often more that is produced from business earnings. Financing plays an important role at this stage by ensuring growth plans can be implemented.

When it is time to quit, sellers typically want as much cash as they can get. In most cases, this is only possible by working to accommodate the needs of a buyer who may need to borrow a portion of the business price.

In each instance, using financing provides entrepreneurs with financial leverage. This has the potential to boost the overall return. For these reasons financing and business acquisitions, operation and dispositions are inseparable.

Capitalization Rates

The term *capitalization rate* refers to the rate at which a stream of future payments converts into a present value. The concept is also called the "cap rate" or simply "CAP." In any case it is expressed as a rate, like interest. For example, an investment capable of producing $1,000 of income capitalized at 10% indicates a present value of $10,000. As the cap rate declines, the value of the investment increases: conversely, increasing it reduces the size of investment indicated. Consider the following examples:

> $1,000 (income) ÷ 10% (cap) = $10,000 (value)
>
> $1,000 (income) ÷ 8.5% (cap) = $11,764.07 (value)
>
> $1,000 (income) ÷ 1.5% (cap) = $8,695.65 (value)

Investors who expect lower prices and greater value select higher cap rates. Buyers use higher cap rates that indicate lower investment requirements. Investors and ownership both use a capitalization rate to measure the current performance of a business. It can help set expectations of performance, such as, "The business plan for next year offers ownership a 7% rate of return." Or it can be used to value a business when introduced with income into a valuation formula.

Notice how the capitalization formula could be used to incorporate business income (I), value (V), and a rate of return (R) expected. The latter is the capitalization rate.

Selecting a Cap Rate

There are many ways to choose a capitalization rate for investment and valuation, and it is a very important decision.

The cap rate is used repeatedly to compare all business investments under consideration. Investors who focus on small publicly traded companies often establish a capitalization rate as the prime lending rate plus 12 percentage points. Using this approach with a current prime rate of 8.75%, the applicable capitalization rate is 20.75%. When the earnings per share of stock are divided by this amount, the value they will pay is indicated.

Venture capitalists invest in small businesses. They typically do not want to involve themselves with management, however, and are only concerned with ROI (return on investment). Their capitalization rate may be less, prime plus 6% or 14.75%, but their package of support comes with other benefits. Generally, in exchange for providing growth capital, they have options to acquire ownership for a very favorable price. Their investment horizon is five to seven years, at which time they like to sell their interest to the original ownership. The price paid will be based on the increased value of the company. In the event management is successful, the investment is lucrative. If, however, management fails to meet well-defined performance objectives, the venture capitalists can take control of the board – thus control of the company – and sell it to recover their original investment.

Angel capital investors work like venture capitalists but typically may be less aggressive. Their formulas differ to the extent that their target business investments and commitments of capital are often smaller. They frequently provide management with consulting assistance as well, which helps to ensure the company stays on track (since the original ownership is also serving as management and the potential for distractions is high). Angel capital investors are not, however, given the sweet name because they are more generous. They typically expect investment terms and capitalization rates on par with their venture capital cousins.

Commercial banks are the most frequent user of capitalization rates. They have the closest and most frequent association with the small business sector. They invest money in these entities in the form of loans for acquisition and expansion. The interest rate charged on money loaned is the bank's return on investment.

A bank's capitalization rate is derived from their cost of money and cost of doing business. Combined these produce what is known as the prime rate of interest – the rate charged to the bank's customers. Small business borrowers often pay the bank a few percentage points of interest over the prime lending rate, so that is the bank's capitalization rate. This can be a good benchmark for entrepreneurs to use when selecting a capitalization rate for business investing.

Using a Cap Rate in Valuations

Use of capitalization rates when valuing a business are helpful but of limited value. They seldom take into consideration the differences between EBIT, EBITDA and business cash flow. In addition, they fail to account for the effects of financing on earnings. It takes money to pay off debt, which should come from business cash flow. Consequently value is often indicated using the premise that debt does not exist, which is seldom true (most businesses are acquired or expanded by securing additional financing to pay the cost). The costs of servicing debt will reduce free cash flow. Actually, in some cases it will be nearly eliminated, as free cash flow is redirected from the entrepreneur to the bank. However, paying off a loan instead of paying a return to investors can be a lucrative business strategy. There can be additional benefits created by amortization of debt.

Financing for Leverage

Some entrepreneurs believe nirvana is a no-money-down business acquisition. (This can be true.) Others feel the best situation is business ownership with no debt. After years of paying off a bank loan, the lure of debt-free status is very appealing. While not a mistake, such a capital structure does not always maximize the earning potential of a business. Under the right conditions, financing will enhance, even multiply, a return on investment. This is true because of the principal of financial, or investment, leverage.

Leverage in business ownership is a way to increase the return *without increasing ownership's investment* or equity. In fact, these are often reduced when investment leverage is used. Create investment leverage by adding debt to the capital structure of a business. The combination of remaining equity and new debt may produce a larger result than the equity could have created by itself. More important, the return on equity can increase – sometimes very impressively.

For example, if an entrepreneur with $50,000 in cash wants to buy a business, there are various options to consider. Buying a business for $50,000 is one. Another is to buy a larger business for $100,000, using the same $50,000 of cash plus an additional $50,000 of borrowed equity – a loan. This is called "leveraging the acquisition" since the equity is leveraged two-to-one: one dollar of equity controls two dollars of business assets. The prevailing mantra of most entrepreneurs "More sooner is better," makes leveraging acquisitions more appealing – so most involve some type of financing. As a result, leverage may improve the return on investment. This occurs when the cost to borrow money is less than the return provided from the investment.

Assume a $100,000 business has free cash flow of $35,000. If the business has no debt, this provides ownership with a 35% return on investment ($35,000/$100,000 = 35%). Now, imagine a strategy to examine the benefits of investment leverage is considered. Assume $50,000 is borrowed for seven years at 8.75% interest. The monthly payments are $798.12, or $9,577.50 annually. Money used to service the debt is taken from free cash flow of $35,000. The remaining free cash flow ($25,422.50) is the new return to the investor. Equity on the other hand is reduced from $100,000 to $50,000. The new return to ownership will be calculated as:

$25,422.50 (Investment) ÷ $50,000 (equity) = 51% (return)

The result is obvious. Return to the investor has increased from 35% to 51%. That's a 45.7% increase in the rate of return from this business. And although the IRV formula substitutes equity for value here, it is still a valid comparison since the original value was the same as equity – $100,000. Keep in mind that ownership following this strategy also has $50,000 of borrowed cash to use in any way they wish. Many will invest in another enterprise.

This example clearly illustrates how leverage is created to maximize the earning power of a business in relation to ownership's equity. Can it be taken too far? Absolutely. The LBO's of the late 20th century are good examples. Investors were so aggressive, they attempted to finance entire purchase prices using no equity.

It will be shown in future sections describing leveraged cash flow methods of valuation (Chapter 10) how leveraged buyouts can be structured. For the moment, remember consistent cash flows combined with favorable earnings trends are prerequisites to highly leveraged acquisitions. This is because servicing debt can require most if not all free cash flow. Should earnings decline, owners are faced with the unhappy proposition of supporting business debt from personal reserves. The risk of failure is high because the margin for error is so small.

Despite the caution, to exercise leveraging a business responsibly remains a money-making tool for entrepreneurs. To improve success, there are certain aspects of financing to understand and use with versatility: debt coverage ratio, loan-to-value ratio and amortization. A discussion of each follows.

Debt Coverage Ratio

Lenders use two basic devices to limit their exposure to loss from small business loans. One limit, a debt coverage ratio, is based on business free cash flow. (The other, a loan-to-value ratio, is based on collateral and will be discussed later.)

A debt coverage ratio (DCR) is used to discount the amount of free cash flow that can be applied to payment of debt requested. This safeguard is intended to ensure that enough cash remains available to service debt even if earnings decrease. Used in this way, the DCR is a barometer reflecting the perceived risk associated with the business cash flow of the borrower.

Usually DCR and risk move up or down in relationship to each other. (The only exception is if DCR falls below 1.00 which, as a practical matter, does not occur.) There are few standards established for leaders to measure risk and assign a DCR. It is not, however, entirely arbitrary. Borrower's credit history and proven management skill, stability of business earnings, liquidity of collateral – all are important considerations. Environmental forces can also play a role, which is particularly evident when stiff competition for the borrower's business makes an appearance. So, the DCR is a subjective measurement of risk.

DCR's are generally between 1.00 and 1.50. When used to discount a cash flow, the latter is divided by the former. In the business XYZ Company example used throughout this text, free cash flow is $19,932. This is money that could be treated as a return on investment for the cash investor or for payment on debt, or both. For simplicity assume a 100% conversion to retire debt. Assume the lender has, based on experience, selected a debt coverage ratio of 1.10. The amount of annual debt service (ADS) that can be paid will be $18,120. This is calculated as follows:

$19,932 ÷ 1.10 (DCR)= $18,120 (Annual Debt Service)

Examine the table below to more fully understand the potential impact of DCR on annual debt service:

FCF	$19,932	$19,932	$19,932	$19,932	$19,932
DCR	1.00	1.20	1.30	1.40	1.50
ADS	$19,932	$16,610	$15,332	$14,237	$13,288

It is easy to see the impact of DCR. One-third of the business's free cash flow is eliminated for use as annual debt service (ADS) where the DCR is high. As a result, the amount of potential investment leverage is reduced. The DCR, then, is an important chess piece in the game of negotiating financing.

Loan-to-Value Ratios

A second device lenders use to limit exposure is a loan-to-value ratio (LTV). The loan-to-value ratio ties the amount that can be borrowed to the fair market value of assets available for collateral. For example, conventional home mortgages frequently have an LTV of 80%. This means the lending institution will loan the borrower up to 80% of the fair market value of the property as determined by an appraisal. Thus, a home valued at $100,000 with an 80% LTV would qualify for an $80,000 mortgage.

Banks use LTVs to guard against loss of capital. If the borrower defaults on the loan, the collateral should be enough, when sold, to satisfy the remaining balance due. Take note, if the remaining loan balance is greater than the net proceeds collected from assets sold, the borrower is still responsible for paying the difference. For this reason, smart entrepreneurs attempt to negotiate "non-recourse" notes, which exempt them from such personal liability. In any event, commercial lenders know collection is an uncertain reality when a business defaults on a loan. The LTV helps prevent such losses if an entrepreneur is forced to fold.

Loan-to-value ratios are important to consider when exploring the financing option of a small business. Like their companion – DCR – they reduce the amount of leverage to an acquisition. It is important to be familiar with use of LTVs. They will apply to almost every business loan made by institutional lenders and these are another chess piece to move.

There are several categories of business assets that may be used as collateral for a business loan. Real estate, furnishings/fixtures/equipment, inventory and intellectual capital all have a different lifespan. Their liquidity varies, too.

Applying a 100% LTV would be almost unheard of. It is more reasonable to expect LTVs for these asset classes will fall with a range roughly described as follows:

Real Estate	75% to 90%
Furnishings/Fixtures/Equipment	50% to 75%
Inventory	25% to 50%
Intellectual Capital	0% to 25%

These are estimated ranges only and may vary from lender to lender, locale to locale and business to business. Also, keep in mind banks will seldom (if ever) offer financing using intellectual capital as collateral.

Amortization

Amortization was described earlier as an accounting charge to income based on the periodic reduction of an intangible asset's original value. A second definition is the payoff of debt through regularly timed payments of principal and interest. Payments to principal represent equal increases in equity if business value remains constant. Payments to interest are treated as deductible expenses.

Amortization of debt is useful to business valuation. After a DCR and LTV have been selected, it is possible to estimate the amount of debt a business can borrow. Calculating the amortization of the debt helps entrepreneurs create ways a business can afford the financing available. This will be come evident in the leveraged cash flow method of valuation. Using amortization as a financing tool emphasizes the entrepreneur's ability to anticipate DCRs and LTVs, as well as calculate loan terms, interest rates, present value, future value and periodic payments on debt projected. This is the structure of financing and has a direct bearing on the benefits financial leverage is intended to create.

The introduction of inexpensive financial calculators (with amortizing functions) vastly simplified the calculation of payments on debt. These instruments break the amortization calculation into five variables: term, interest, payment, present value and future value. With these calculators it is possible to enter any four variables and easily solve for the fifth.

Term. Term refers to the length of time that will pass from the origination of the loan to the payoff date. There is a general rule to follow when estimating loan terms: Don't make long-term loans on short-term assets. Otherwise, the loan will remain unpaid long after the collateral asset has experienced function or economic obsolescence or both. The lender's risk will be unacceptable.

The term of a loan should be less than and no more than the useful life of the asset. Here is a general list of loan terms to use with business assets often financed, subject to regional and individual variances:

Real Estate	5 to 30 years
Furnishings/Fixtures/Equipment	3 to 7 years
Inventory	I/O or 0 to 3 Years
Intellectual Capital	N/A

I/O stands for interest only. Sometimes banks will finance and inventory using a line of credit loan. In these cases the borrower may only interest on the balance financed followed by periodic reductions in principal. There is no term. Since banks seldom loan on intellectual capital, no term is stated.

When entering the term of a loan into a financial calculator, it may be requested as *n,* which stands for the number of payments that will be made throughout the term. If monthly payments are called for *n* is the term of the loan in years times twelve.

Interest. Interest is the cost of using money that is expressed as a rate for a period of time. The period is typically annual. As mentioned earlier, monthly payments will include interest and principal. These are calculated roughly as the interest due on the outstanding balance of the loan for the previous or coming month plus principal. The principal is the difference between the payment amount and the interest payment.

It is easy to see the interest portion of payments that occur early in the loan term will be larger than those occurring late in the loan life. This is why the same payment schedule will retire less debt early and more debt later. Many investors counteract this slow reduction of loan principal with a simple technique by making the current payment plus the small principal payment that would be due with next month's installment as they advance their amortization schedule one month. When this occurs, the interest that would have been paid is cancelled, too. Done consistently this provides a substantial savings of interest and reduces the loan term by 50%.

For more information about how interest rates are determined, see "Capitalization Rates" earlier in this chapter. Banks charge small business borrowers 1% to 3% over their prime-lending rate. Interest is either fixed or variable. If fixed, it will remain constant for a specified portion (if not the entire term) of the loan; if variable, it can change periodically based on pre-set limits (i.e., a change of no more than 1% increase or decrease per period with a maximum cap of not more than 5% over the life of the loan). A debt with a flexible rate such as this is called an adjustable rate mortgage, or ARM.

Present value. The present value of the loan is the amount borrowed. It is determined from the borrower's need or request when adjusted by the LTV, DCR, interest rate and term. A capitalization rate is used to measure the present value of a stream of payments to be collected in the future.

Future Value. The future value of a loan amortization is the amount of principal outstanding on the payoff date of the loan. At that time the loan balance will be zero if a loan is "fully amortized." This means the payments are enough to pay off the entire loan during the term.

In some cases, where cash flow considerations are a greater priority, equal monthly payments may not be sufficient to pay off the entire loan by the end of the loan term. An outstanding balance will be due, called a "balloon payment." In the world of finance it is common to receive a loan with an amortization term where the actual payoff of the loan from monthly payments would not occur until long after the payoff date. Loans are frequently amortized for 15 years but due in five. In this case the term of the loan is five years.

Payment. The fifth variable in the amortizing equation is the amount of money needed each period to reduce the principal as agreed during the loan term at the specified interest rate. Payments may occur monthly, quarterly, semi-annually or annually. They may be amortizing or include a fixed amount of principal each month plus interest on the outstanding balance.

Chapter 6
Measuring Business RPM (Risk/Price Multiple)

A risk/price multiple (RPM) is often called a "pricing multiple." It is a yardstick entrepreneurs use to quantify the risk and value of a business. Used in this way it helps compare acquisition candidates. One can quickly measure the value from the risk that is indicated.

A risk/price multiple is used in the excess earnings method of business valuation, but it can also function as a guide to management since it will illustrate a business's weaknesses and strengths. It can be used to help determine management compensation bonuses, too.

Risk/price multiples are more commonly used, however, as quick estimates of business value because they are so simple. For example, a business with a higher multiple is perceived as a better business than one with a lower multiple. This means the risk is less, so the value is more.

The risk/price multiple appears in many valuation rules of thumb, too. These take the form of "five times earnings," or "one and a half times revenue" and so forth. Formulas using an RPM can be quick and helpful indicators of value if developed from sound premises. Unfortunately this is not always the case.

Consider a most common multiple, "five times earnings." Business owners seeking to dispose of their business property are notorious for selecting very high multiples. Values indicated may not offer investors enough cash flow to compensate management, provide a return on investment or service acquisition debt. The price indicated can be so high it is laughable. Buyers work in reverse. They prefer a multiple so low it would be possible to finance 100% of an acquisition from free cash flow. The business is probably worth more than their highly leveraged estimate of value.

To further confuse the use of multiples, no clear definition is often given to the type of earnings used with the multiple. Is it EBIT, EBITDA, cash flow or free cash flow? Clearly EBIT and free cash flow will produce very different values using the same RPM. One must also question selection of the variable "5." Is it a function of the owners' desire to sell for more than the business is worth, the buyers' interest in paying less than they should, or comparative market criteria? The latter option sounds most credible but only if RPM's used are developed from an accurate set of "comps." There is a better way.

Consider building an RPM using intrinsic business elements in addition to these other methods. Comparative data, seller expectations and buyer demands are balanced with business indicators of performance as predictors of value. These may limit the RPM's ability to produce a reliable result, too. Developing a risk/price multiple from external *and internal* characteristics is a better way. It takes more time and investigation, but the tool created is useful and meaningful enough to more than justify the effort.

Many Kinds of Risk to Measure

Risk in business is the possibility of losing value or failing to increase value. There are many kinds of risk: appreciation risk, inflation risk, interest rate risk, inventory risk, liquidity risk, political risk, repayment risk or risk of principal.

While all types of risk are important to small business entrepreneurs, appreciation, inventory, liquidity, repayment and risk of principal are of greatest concern to them.

Appreciation risk pertains to the ability of the business to gain in value. There are many reasons this can occur. Some are beyond the control of ownership, others are not. Recall, amortization applies responsible financial leverage to produce a gradual increase in ownership equity. This occurs as debt is reduced. The potential gain available, though desirable, remains finite however. Appreciation, on the other hand, offers infinite potential for increases in business value. Effective management of financial leverage combined with gradual appreciation has the potential to create impressive wealth over time. It also reduces the risk to principal.

Liquidity risk is created by the possibility the business will run out of cash. Professor Fran Jabara, founder of the center for Entrepreneurship at Wichita State University, says, "Rule #1: Never run out of cash. Rule #2: Never, ever, run out of cash." The reason is, quite simply, when a business is out of cash, it is out of options. When options to carry on are removed, the business can easily fail.

Inventory risk is capturing increased attention. Dell Computer enjoys a commanding lead in the computer manufacturing industry due, in part, to their successful system of inventory management. With sales of $18 million per day, they only have a one-week supply of inventory on hand. Dramatic levels of functional and economic obsolescence constantly occurring in the hardware industry create great risk. Millions invested in stagnant inventory does not enhance business performance. Dell's unique approach to inventory management reduces this risk considerably.

Building a Risk/Price Multiple

As indicated, several factors affect development of a useful risk/price multiple. It is not possible to produce a perfect indicator of performance. The process is subjective: it's determined by the perceptions of the person conducting the analysis. With good material from a complete due diligence, the analyst can develop an RPM that is highly defensible.

To calculate a risk/price multiple, the following approach is recommended. Separate the business into six categories: finance, control, marketing, sales, production and service. Notice they correspond to those recommended in a due diligence investigation.

Each category is assigned a value from 0 to 5 (see below). Category values are the average of five subcategories representing characteristics of that category. These subcategories receive a value of from 0 to 5, too. With both categories and subcategories, high numbers indicate better quality and less risk whereas lower numbers mean low quality and greater risk. When selecting values for each category or subcategory, it may be helpful to use the following scale for easy reference:

SCALE OF VALUES TO MEASURE BUSINESS RPM

0 MAXIMUM RISK. Business out of control. Failure is likely.

1 HIGH RISK. Loss of equity likely. Crisis management prevails.

2 RISKY. Small margins for error, but recovery is possible.

3 ACCEPTABLE RISK. Market and management forces can prevail.

4 LOW RISK. Good control over growth and equity. Secure.

5 MINIMAL RISK. Excellent control, many opportunities and profitable.

The seven category values are averaged, and the answer is the business risk/price multiple – its RPM – and an indicator of value derived from factors internal to and forces external to the business. Here, together with thoughts to consider and questions to ask, are the categories and subcategories used to develop the risk/price multiple. The long-form RPM calculator can be found in the Appendix Section. The short form follows:

Business RPM
XYZ Company

1. Finance	3.0
2. Control	3.0
3. Marketing	1.0
4. Sales	2.0
5. Production	4.0
6. Service	4.0
7. Intellectual Capital	1.0
Total	18.0
Variables	÷7
Business RPM	2.57

Finance

Trailing Revenue. Emphasis is on historical trends. Is revenue increasing each year, holding steady or declining? Normally, steadily increasing revenues are signs of a well-run business. In this case, risk would be low so the value selected would be greater. Risk is low, so the multiple is high.

Declining revenue is usually an indication of less demand for the business output of goods and services. It could also be related to limited production capability. This deserves careful study; however, declining revenue is always a strong indicator of greater business risk.

Do not always consider rapid increases in revenue as favorable developments. Growth is the hardest part of a business to manage. Growth requires increases in capital spending to support production. If demand suddenly stops after significant investments in infrastructure have been made, cash reserves may run dry. Risk is increased.

Revenue Momentum. Significant annual improvements in business revenue are generally extrapolated into continuing increases called *momentum*. Determining how much momentum, translated as increased revenue, will occur next year and the year after is more difficult. This involves forecasting, which is challenging and uncertain. Unlike risk, uncertainty cannot be adequately measured.

History remains the best predictor of the future. Provided the forces that feed increases in trailing revenues remain viable, one might extrapolate continuing changes of the same, greater or lesser degree. Companies with higher momentum supported by premises expected to remain in place have less risk and a higher value. Companies with no momentum or reverse momentum have a high risk and are assigned a low value.

Capital Structure. How financially fit is the business? To determine a value for this subcategory, examine business debt and equity. When debt is more than double equity (using market value of assets), the business is highly leveraged. Risk is greater. Conversely, a business with no debt may not be risk free. It may have a lower ROI. A capital structure can also be a sign management complacency exists. Missing marketing opportunities could be occurring repeatedly. If the business is not keeping pace, a growth wall may have been built or may be under construction. The business may not be able to handle debt. Risk could be greater. Look closely.

Leverage Opportunities. Recall one tactic to increase return occurs with financial leverage. Businesses with no debt, as just described, may not enjoy the opportunity to create financial leverage. Their risk is greater since their return is lower. More importantly, financial leverage may be required to keep pace with the market. If it is not affordable, risk is greater. Businesses that can employ financial leverage to improve ROI, or to stay ahead of competitors, enjoy less risk and a higher value.

Earnings and Cash Flow. Clearly, those businesses with cash flow sufficient to accomplish ownership objectives are most desirable. The presence of cash increases access to more strategies. More available strategies extend the life and profitability of a business. Ample cash flows reduce risk; limited cash flow increases risk.

Control

Employee Turnover Rates and Costs. The inability to hire and retain quality employees can put a company out of business. The rate of turnover among employees is a reflection of job fit. One wrests control of business functions from management by forcing the focus on to replacing and retraining people; the other seizes control of business earnings. This is a crucial consideration in a tight labor market, which many experts say will continue for the next 10 to 15 years.

Employee turnover rates are calculated as the number of employees leaving each year, for whatever reason, as a percentage of the total people employed. The national average hovers around 16%, which means 16% of the people that are employed today will be gone one year from today. Most companies discover their rate is as high as 30%. Turnover reduces management control.

Employee turnover costs are also much higher than most expect. It is not uncommon for the indirect and direct costs of employee turnover to exceed an employee's annual salary.

Both employee turnover rates and costs are a threat to management's control. Examine how the business addresses the issue of job fit and environment to encourage longevity. Aggressive measures reduce risk. If no measures are in place to deal with this hidden menace, risk is greater.

Employee Compensation. Nothing motivates people like having a piece of the pie. Nothing demoralizes employees faster than being treated unfairly. To resolve both, management may install a written, company-wide, compensation policy. When in writing, trust is improved and people will perceive management as more fair. When incentives to perform behaviors that lead to improved financial results are in place, people are rewarded with validation and money. If these are delivered in amounts that are comparable with employment alternatives, the system will be productive. Risk is less.

Contingency Planning. Considerable emphasis has been given to the subject of business planning. Hal Geneen summarizes business planning very well with a three sentence-course on how to run a business. "You read a book from beginning to end. You run a business the opposite way. You start with the end and do everything you must to reach it." Does the business have a financial plan with a revenue and expense forecast? If so, risk is a little less. Does the business have a Plan "B" or "C" in the event Plan "A" fails to produce? It is certain at least part of the original plan won't work. Options reduce risk.

Another factor affecting control and contingency planning is management's flow of control. Ownership that supports management by committee or chain of command are outmaneuvered and outrun by aggressive competition. Reactions are slow and often occur when it is too late. Risk is greater.

Absence of a reaction plan also increases risk. Because business moves so fast, companies must be in position to react swiftly. Unpredictable changes occur almost daily. How well developed is the company's ability to react to constant unpredictability? A good reaction plan may be the best way to reduce risk to control in the fast-paced world of e-commerce. Risk would be less. In the absence of a reaction, strategic operating or financial plan, risk is higher.

Network Penetration. A company that builds a product that can be used by only one person is not penetrating the network of consumers available. A company that builds a product that can be used by more than one person does a better job. A company that builds a product, such as meaningful information sent by e-mail, that can be read by one million people enjoys exciting network penetration. With greater network penetration, risk is less. With no network penetration, how can the business keep pace with businesses that have developed this resource?

Potential Litigation. Every business can be subject to claims from customers and competitors. Does the business have a history or lawsuits? Is there any pending litigation? Are there any outstanding judgments? One measure of exposure to litigation is activity that draws fire. Another measure is how well a company builds a defensive shield to prevent the impact of litigation should it occur. When the record shows a history of lawsuits, the risk is high. Where there are none and counter-measures are in place, risk is less.

Marketing

Well-defined Marketing Plan. Does the company have a written marketing plan? The ability to follow the plan to identify core values of the company with those of its target market is the key link to sales. With no plan to define and execute marketing risk is very high. With a well-executed plan, risk is reduced.

Branded Power. A brand exists to create trust. To do that it must be memorable and memorizable. It has to be delivered frequently and consistently to produce results. On the Internet, a company's brand is its substitute for the bricks and mortar of a business. Companies that successfully brand themselves will have less risk in the future compared to those that don't.

Market Differentiation. Risk to a business will increase if it cannot differentiate itself from competitors. A business must be able to tell customers why it is different and why it is better. If it cannot, there is no reason for customers to patronize one business over another. When differentiation is effective, however, risk can be reduced.

Market Segmentation. One does not need to sell his or her products and services to everyone in the world to be successful – just to everyone with a need for what is offered. Kellogg *Grape Nuts* is a breakfast cereal that sells to just 2% of the total breakfast cereal market and that small share of the market is worth $160 million a year. Because of this effective market segmentation, *Grape Nuts* is a 100-year old company (that doesn't even sell grapes or nuts). Companies that do not know who their target market or market segment is, and therefore fail to attract them, have greater risk.

E-commerce Activity. Companies that have no plan to participate in e-commerce activity have the greatest risk. It doesn't matter if they can't deliver a hamburger in cyberspace – they can use the medium to attract customers. It is said that companies with no e-commerce function will become extinct, and soon.

Sales

Type of Service/Product. Understanding the physical characteristics of a product or service is not enough to eliminate risk. One must understand what is offered in terms of its transactional, consultative or enterprise characteristics. One is a soft drink, the other is advice and the latter is a partnership. Failure to recognize these differences and how they are changing create greater risk.

Sales Process Fit. Among the most common mistakes made in sales is the mismatch of sales technique, or process, to product type. The sales process must improve the value of the product. Otherwise, it should be eliminated entirely so the product can enjoy greater price/competitive advantages. And more sales. When a mismatch occurs, the cost of sales is too high in relation to the results received. And risk is higher.

Sales Incentives Available. Ross Perot is a billionaire. So was Ewing Kauffman. Both were salespeople whose management limited their earning capability. Both quit their jobs and started their own companies for the wide-open territory of entrepreneurship. Are the business's salespeople given incentives that treat them like employees or like entrepreneurs? The latter reduces business risk.

Sales Training Programs. As with advertising, when business turns unfavorable the training budget is often cut first. This does not lead to improved results. The existence of training programs in a company reduces risk. The use of them at the right time reduces it more.

Wired Distribution. The no-brainer of the 21st century is distributing services via the Internet. The gains one can make in time, flexibility and costs are worth more over the long term than the development costs. As is previously stated, a close association with Internet commerce reduces risk.

Production

Emphasis on Quality. "Quality costs when you don't have it." In the absence of quality, errors will increase. This is not a new concept – it was originally introduced by William Edwards Demming as the Demming management method. The premise of this system is simple: More errors result in greater production costs and lower earnings. That increases risk. What steps in the flow of production and service are taken to ensure quality maintains high?

Innovation. In business one is either moving forward or backward. This is because standing still permits a business to fall behind compared to others sustaining forward motion. The difference between which directions a business moves has its genesis in its innovative spirit. Even the Industrial Age suggestion box is an attempt to find new ideas. Employees, who see all the problems in a business first hand, have the innovative solutions needed to remove them. In the fast-paced world of business today, how well management draws out this innovative element will affect business risk favorably or unfavorably.

Capacity vs. Demand. If business has the ability to produce more than it delivers, risk to revenue is less. This is, provided there is a growing demand for products and services produced. Companies without the capacity meet demand are growing, but also have greater risk to their survival.

Obsolescence. It has been shown obsolescence, whether functional or economic, is a loss of asset value. Risk to principal increases in the face of obsolescence. Examine production process and equipment for obsolescence. It is a direct measure of business risk.

Inventory Management. It was mentioned previously that Dell Computer company has used sound principles of inventory management to reduce risk. Another device is access to inventory. Examine how well the business maximizes its ability to order, receive and manage inventory. Those who do it most efficiently, for the least amount of investment, have the least risk.

Service

Customer Satisfaction. This is an intangible asset that money cannot buy. Good impressions on the part of customers are hard to earn. They are easy to keep so long as service is maintained. If lost, satisfaction takes years to rebuild. The analyst should take the time to interview a few customers of the business and attempt to determine their level of satisfaction. If the business is well thought of, risk is less.

Employee Recognition. Pay is not a motivator. Recognition from a peer group is more powerful. Businesses who recognize this important concept offer programs that recognize superior achievement. Employees respond with superior performance. When employees are recognized for their hard work the risk is less.

Team Spirit. Peter Drucker has said a management team is one of the most powerful new tools in the manager's toolbox. Teams assigned to specific functions have the potential to produce more results, as a unit, than the team members functioning individually. Teams help businesses reduce risk.

Flexibility. Stellar service in small businesses is often linked to flexibility. It can be their greatest strength when facing larger competitors who are often unable to quickly adapt to marketplace changes. As a result growth walls are less likely to develop in a small entrepreneurial company. Their search for new ideas is constant. When found they are quickly put to use. Flexibility and adaptability reduce risk.

Open Communication. Employees, customers and associates represent a rich source of feedback. This information has the potential to offer the most valuable service improvements a company can achieve. Companies that encourage communication from all sources have less chance of losing touch with the marketplace – and less risk.

Intellectual Capital

Integrated Vision. The old saw still applies: It is easier to cross the country with a map and a destination than by wandering aimlessly about. Without a vision of where the business is headed, uncertainty can prevail in the minds of customers, employees, investors and professional representatives. Being a winner means knowing what winning means. Everyone wants to hitch his or her wagon to a winner.

Vision inspires. Vision motivates. Look for signs the vision is integrated into the everyday thinking of employees and customers. This improves retention and results. It is the foundation of quality service. With no vision, crisis management can prevail and risk is higher.

Employee Motivation. Are employees given an environment where they can do whatever is necessary to produce results? Is this type of autonomy encouraged? These forces, combined with others, build employee motivation. Try to imagine a business succeeding when the employees don't care. The risk will be very high.

Potent Synergies. This occurs when combined expenses produce a result that is greater than the two expenses treated separately. Synergy is the basis for many business mergers. Operating costs for the new entity are lower while revenues and earnings increase. Synergies are easy to find but hard to make work, however. In fact, many companies that grow by acquisition discover in the final analysis, the cost did not outweigh the benefits. Still, the presence of synergy among categories considered in the risk/price multiple can reduce risk.

Key People. Management and people are important assets in a business. Unfortunately, some expect to be treated in a manner that is disproportionate to their value. Look for redundancy in job functions; does more than one person know how to perform a critical skill? Where this exists, risk resulting from the loss of a key employee is less. Where it exists, risk is less.

Institutional Intelligence. Coca-Cola has a secret formula. Microsoft has a source code. Who can argue the value of this institutional intelligence has propelled both to roles as corporate leaders on a global scale. Intelligence is the product of the new economy. As with people, businesses can have trade secrets that represent a rich source of intellectual capital. These are patents, copyrights, production processes or consumer intelligence. When properly leveraged these intangible assets can provide a distinctive competitive edge. That reduces risk. When all competitors are able to the do the same thing, risk is greater.

The subcategories suggested for use in calculating a business RPM may vary. Investor interests, business types and market conditions can cause this to occur. Flexibility is an important component of business valuation. Entrepreneurs building business risk/price multiples may elect to make substitutions to better suit their need.

In addition, the work to create a business RPM can become as detailed as one chooses to make it. Clearly, to develop precise information about each subcategory might require extensive investigation. However, values assigned remain a subjective interpretation of the entrepreneur or valuation analyst. So while investigation is a healthy exercise, one can reach a point of diminishing return.

By all means, perform a complete due diligence. Or as complete as time and resources permit. Then step away, adopt a fresh perspective and quickly evaluate or score each subcategory. Then calculate the business RPM. As before, first impressions based on good data most often prove correct.

Chapter 7
Accurate Variables Produce Reliable Values

Business valuation techniques extrapolate value from a combination of intrinsic and extrinsic factors. Interpreting and distilling them into selected variables makes it possible to calculate business value. The variables are then used in the valuation formulas. Therefore, business values estimated are only as good as the data.

Collect lots of information. For example, RPM is used in the excess earnings method of valuation. At a first glance, it appears to be a lot of work to develop this variable. However, at the option of the analyst, RPM can be useful in both leveraged cash flow methods of business valuation, too. RPM is created from the entrepreneur's assessment of qualities of a business and its marketplace. That does not occur without a broad base of data to consider. Subjective impressions also improve with additional data. When combined, different approaches to determining value improve the accuracy of the valuation estimate.

Despite the fact that entrepreneurs rely on facts and impressions, the surest way to produce a superior result is with continued refinement. This is accomplished when each variable is built on a logical premise. For instance, one can know EBIT is reliable because it is specifically calculated in the business books (which are either an authentic record of business activity or a gross misrepresentation). Likewise, cash flow results from a step-by-step reconstruction of actual earnings and expenses. There is a logical basis for adjusting EBIT. And so it goes. Intelligent premises such as these are used to develop business variables and values.

Resist the temptation to revisit and adjust variables up or down simply to validate an expectation. Thus trouble begins. It can occur when a lower than expected value estimate disappoints business principals - after so many years of effort, their reaction is understandable. In the alternative, buyers can use inaccurate variables to create an unrealistic offer, which only alienates a seller and stops communication. When either happens, the tail is wagging the dog. A successful outcome is the signature of a competent business valuation.

As the valuation process moves forward a sense of the business's value begins to emerge. Variables get nailed down, so less is left to question. Eventually a point is reached where there is little or nothing left to calculate ... or to chance. Then business realities dictate business value and, to the extent possible, subjectivity is removed from the analyst's final measurement. That is the goal.

When all variables that drive valuation formulas are correct, the resulting value is more likely to be equally correct. Uncertainty declines and risk is reduced. A buyer doesn't overspend, and a seller doesn't take a loss. This is possible when the numbers speak for themselves.

Challenge Hybrids with Alternatives

One need not learn all the valuation techniques in creation to do an efficient job. However, learning enough from a few proven formulas to recognize the flaws of hybrid techniques is a helpful act of self-preservation. Many hybrids exist only to fulfill a specific purpose – supporting ownership's estimate of business value. Quite often that estimate is based on what a seller "wants" and not on what a business is actually "worth." To the untrained eye, with no logical basis for disagreement, hybrids can be impressive and seductive solutions. But trouble often lurks behind a veil of confidence and propriety. Challenge hybrid valuations with alternative techniques before accepting their conclusions.

Consider the following hybrid valuation formula applied to the example presented earlier in this text. The ownership here believes business value is a derivative of three things: return on investment, a pricing multiple and sales volume. When organized into the hybrid formula proposed, calculation of value occurs in three logical steps.

STEP 1: Determine the return on investment (ROI) from EBIT and Equity. From the example, this can be expressed in the calculation follows:

$20,920 ÷ $65,681.64 = 32% (return on investment)

STEP 2: Calculate an applicable revenue multiple. The following range of multiples is originally offered:

EBIT	Multiple
<20	.75
21 - 30	1.00
>30	1.25✓

STEP 3: Determine the business value. Multiply the applicable multiple by the business revenue. With an ROI of 32%, the pricing multiple is 1.25 and revenue is $608,951.

$608,951 x 1.25 = $761,189

The value therefore is $761,189.

This hybrid valuation formula appears to be logical. But the result should ring an alarm bell of concern for the analyst or buyer. Consider the outcome of this formula. To begin, one must question whether the use of equity is correct. Should it be replaced with assets at market value when adjusted to include only those transferred in a sale? These are the investor's current commitment of resources invested in the enterprise and include inventory ($55,000), land and building ($105,000) and old furnishings ($5,000), for a total of $165,000.

Second, the range for multiples is narrow and limited. This is also a unique combination of values, not common to other valuation techniques.

Next, in a retail company is revenue the best companion to use with a pricing multiple? What occurs if the same approach is taken with a service company (having no cost of goods) whose revenue is the same as the other's gross profit? If the EBIT of both companies were the same, how would their values be different? And if they are, why should they be?

It is possible to resolve some of these concerns by adjusting the formula. Calculating ROI from EBIT and market value of assets is the first step. This means only inventory, land, building and furnishings are considered.

$$\$20,920 \div \$165,000 = 13\% \text{ (return on investment)}$$

Next, enrich the range of multiples to increase the accuracy of the relationship of earnings to pricing multiple.

EBIT	Multiple
<5 to 10	.75
11 to15	.875
16 to 20	1.00
21 to 25	1.125
26 to 30	1.25

The indicated pricing multiple is .875. Finally, by substituting gross profit for revenue, the formula is targeted at income used only to pay expenses and provide earnings. This approach is more universal and can be used for both service and retail establishments. The gross profit of the example is $211,421. Therefore, the business value is calculated as $211,421 times .875 to equal $184,993.38 – vastly different from the earlier value proposed.

To continue exploring which value is more accurate, notice two important considerations: the price paid for goodwill, and the influence of comparable investments.

Determine the amount of goodwill included in each price. Using the earlier amount and market value of assets, goodwill is figured as follows:

A. $761,189 (value) - $165,000 (assets) = $596,189 (goodwill)

vs.

B. $184,993 (value) - $165,000 (assets) = $19,993 (goodwill)

That's 28 times EBIT for the proposed value compared to just less than one times EBIT in the value created by reworking the hybrid. Which is more appealing to an investor? But more importantly, which is more sensible?

For the answer, review the return available from an investment of $761,189 (the proposed business price) offering an 8.5% return to investors. The interest ($64,701) is three times greater than business EBIT. Nor would an investor need to own or operate the business to receive this reward. Alternative investments such as that described require an investment of $246,111.88 to earn the same return as business EBIT. Roughly one-third of the proposed value produces the same return with less risk and effort. The proprietor's veil of experience and good manners is now transparent – easily penetrated by this analysis.

With investigation, the weakness of hybrid formulas is quickly revealed. As shown, they can be revived with minor modifications. Still, a better test of reliability is to perform valuation calculations using other methods. This will be done as tests of this hybrid's accuracy are performed using valuation techniques presented in this text. Which value, $761,189 or $184,993, is supported by other standards of measurement? For best results, depend on formulas that are universally applicable. They should have proven themselves reasonably accurate over time. And they should offer flexibility so accepted variances in market conditions do not disrupt their otherwise essential, logical premises. Those presented in this text fit these criteria.

A Paradigm: Commercial Real Estate

The approach to business valuation provided here is similar to commercial real estate valuation. At a glance this makes sense because nearly every business has a location, plus every commercial property is held for the production of income and wealth. A business has similar objectives. With the advent of dot.com companies, the similarities of business to commercial real estate may be changing – but slowly. Otherwise they remain very similar. Valuation fundamentals that apply to one can be interpolated and used with the other to produce good results.

There are three basic approaches to estimating the value of commercial property. These are widely accepted techniques used consistently throughout the practice of real estate brokerage, investing and appraising. Approaches to value for commercial land and improvements depend on: 1) market forces in play at the time of valuation, 2) cost to reproduce property under consideration and 3) income or potential income created by the property. Because businesses are so similar to and closely linked with investment real estate, similar valuation approaches have proven effective.

The first such technique is the capitalization method to determine value. It utilizes expected market rates of return from competing investments.

The second is the excess earnings method of valuation – the estimate based on the earning power of tangible and intangible business assets. It is a measure of their cost.

The third valuation technique is income based. A leveraged cash flow method of valuation estimates value by determining the amount of management compensation and debt that can be supported by business income. Two variations are presented so differences in cost of financing available may be considered.

A final estimate of value is a simple or weighted average of four values just mentioned. The methodology is consistent with that used by many real estate appraisers. It can be verified using a confidence index.

Use these valuation formulas together. They are reasonably simple, easy to learn and represent a solution that is, more often than not, adequate and in proportion to the problem at hand.

Keep in mind, also, the example of the hybrid formula just offered. It illustrates how wrong the approach can be. Multiple valuation techniques reveal this discrepancy and therefore improve overall accuracy and confidence. This is another reason the cost, market and income approaches used for commercial real estate are useful with business valuation. The bulk of work to produce a business valuation is in the due diligence. When completed it takes little added effort to run the valuation formulas. Complete them, but the benefits of multiple valuation perspectives are easily retrieved to provide a significant increase in the entrepreneur's performance, profit and wealth.

Chapter 8
The Capitalization Method

The capitalization method of business valuation uses capitalization rates and income to estimate the cash value of a business. Therefore, this value estimate is not a combination of equity and debt. Nor is it presented as a market approach to value in a traditional sense. That typically means comparable sales are used as predictors of value. As explained in the first chapter, data from other businesses sold has limited meaning.

A stronger case could be made for the use of comparable business sales if 1) the sampling of comparables is large enough, 2) markets are similar enough, and 3) the sampling is not out of date. Unfortunately, this seldom occurs. Sales data describing business ownership transfers are normally confidential, the number of potentially qualifying comparable business sales within a given market is likely to be small, and no well-organized reporting facility for each market is in place.

Thus, with this approach market influences on value are derived from rates of return expected by investors and income created within a specific market. These are the primary drivers of value.

The Capitalization Method

The IRV formula is the basis for the capitalization method. In its simplest form I (income), R (rate or cap rate) and V (value) are the variables used. These describe the qualities of an investment. The mathematical expression of this valuation formula is:

$$\frac{I}{R \times V}$$

Knowing any two variables permits someone using this formula to calculate the third:

- I (income) *equals* R (rate) *times* V (value)
- R (rate) *equals* I (income) *divided by* V (value)
- V (value) *equals* I (income) *divided by* R (rate)

Therefore, a buyer who knows the income produced by an investment and the market rate expected could estimate the cash value of the investment. One who knows the rate of return expected and the value, or asking price, can estimate the income that should be available to investors. And knowing the income produced and the value permits calculation of the rate of return available.

Substitution of variables, estimated versus actual, is a feature of this technique that offers impressive flexibility. It can be used to quickly pre-qualify business investments. In most instances an investor seeking to acquire a business will know the asking price and acceptable cap rates. Multiplying one by the other suggests the amount of income that should be available. It will not take much discovery to determine if this is the case. If the actual income is less than estimated, the business may be overpriced. If the income is more than estimated, the business could represent a good value.

An initial calculation of value using the capitalization method permits determining whether the asking price is too high or low. Also, it is possible to calculate a business value expected from actual income. Accomplish this by using actual income and the cap rate expected. Conversely, one could use actual income and asking price to examine the rate of return available.

It is quickly evident that this formula gives the investor a great deal of flexibility to determine, quickly, business value and ROI offered based on business income.

Using Correct Variables

Recall, success in business valuation depends on the correct selection of variables used in the formulas. The capitalization method is no exception. Follow these steps to produce the best results when using the formula.

STEP 1: Select the Correct Income.

Four types of income can be used in the capitalization method: EBIT, EBITDA, cash flow, and free cash flow. In most cases of small business valuation, the income used will be free cash flow – cash flow that has been reconstructed and includes estimated management compensation. Review the earnings summary from the example presented earlier.

STEP 2: Select the Right Rate of Return (Cap Rate).

The earlier discussion of cap rates used in small business valuation indicated several approaches are available to set the rate. There also are several rates to consider. Rates at the time of publication were as follows:

✓ Federal lending rate	5.75%
✓ Prime lending rate (P)	8.75%
✓ Small business lending rate	P +<2.00%
	8.75% to 10.75%
✓ SBA lending rate	P+2.25—2.75%
	11.0% to 11.5%
✓ Safe rate (>5 year CD's)	6.00% to 6.50%

The small business lending rate offered by commercial banks is a good point of beginning. There are many reasons to use it:

- A lender's cap rate is frequently charged by sellers electing to finance the sale of their business. Remember, the interest rate charged to the borrower is the rate of return received by the lender.
- It reflects local market conditions.
- It permits lenders to cover their operating costs and generate a profit.
- It incorporates risk of the investment. The higher the perceptions of risk, the higher the rate.
- The prime rate offered by banks is not affected by changes in business value. At a constant market rate, increases in business income favorably affect business value. The investor's return improves.

For this illustration the cap rate selected is Prime (8.75%) plus 2.75%, or 11.5%.

STEP 3: Calculate the Value.
> Divide the income by the rate. This is the value of the investment indicated. Assume maximum SBA lending rates as applicable investor's capitalization rate.

$$\$19,932 \ (I) \div 11.5\% \ (R) = 173,322 \ (V)$$

From this a business value of $173,322 is indicated. This value, taken from trailing earnings, will provide an investor with an 11.5% return on investment after costs of compensation to management. Entrepreneurs who prefer to operate their business investments would receive management earnings in addition to their return. The combined financial benefit to an operating owner is $50,432. This is how many small business owners perceive and measure the economic reward available to ownership.

The formula for estimating business value using the Capitalization Method looks like this.

$$\frac{\text{INCOME @ \$19,932}}{\text{RATE @ 11.50\% = VALUE @ \$173,322}}$$

As mentioned, the income of an investment is frequently unavailable in the early stages of an entrepreneur's discovery process. Following is an illustration of how using the equation with different variables can produce an alternative value. At a given value of \$173,322 and investor expected ROI of 11.5%, income should be:

$$11.5\% \ (R) \times \$173,322 \ (V) = \$19,932 \ (I)$$

Substituting Variables

If free cash flow is less, the other variables can change. Using business income of \$15,000 with no change in the asking price indicates the rate of return will be 8.65%.

$$\$15,000 \ (I) \div \$173,322 \ (V) = 8.65\% \ (R)$$

The investor has a decision to make. Is the ROI of 8.65% still acceptable, despite its 2.85 actual variance from the market rate chosen? This is also 24.78% less than desired. Or, can the value be adjusted so the desired rate of return is preserved. To calculate the value indicated by the lower income:

$$\$15,000 \ (I) \div 11.5\% \ (R) = \$130,435 \ (V)$$

The new value indicated is \$42,887 less. Adjusting the formula for more income than originally indicated will increase the rate available. To compensate, ownership may elect to raise the value.

$$\$25,000 \ (I) \div \$173,322 \ (V) = 14.42\% \ (R)$$
$$\text{Or}$$
$$\$25,000 \ (I) \div 11.5\% \ (R) = \$217,391 \ (V)$$

Use this simplest of valuation formulas to quickly determine business value. The flexibility of variable substitution permits easy calculation of alternative values and the results they can or should produce. Verify the results with valuation techniques derived from cost and income factors.

Chapter 9
The Excess Earnings Method

As explained earlier, the cost approach to valuing commercial real estate builds on the cost to acquire similar assets. Costs of comparable buildings or improvements, furnishings, fixtures and equipment are combined. The latter may be discounted too for obsolescence observed.

A second valuation technique is easy to learn and use is the excess earnings method. It is similar to a real estate cost approach because adding costs to acquire tangible and intangible property forms the basis for value. The excess earnings method helps define what these are worth if purchased separately, or if alternative properties capable of producing the same economic result were acquired instead. This correlation to asset values differentiates the excess earnings method from other valuation techniques.

The Excess Earnings Method

Excess earnings are business free cash flow less an opportunity cost associated with the market value, or cost, of tangible business assets. The resulting value is an indicator of the cash created by intellectual capital goodwill in a business in excess of value created by the business tangible assets.

The excess earnings method of business valuation is widely used. Although it works well with businesses that are asset intensive, it can also prove useful with service companies where dependence on unique people or assets is high. It's a good approach for small businesses because it quickly separates the value of hard assets from "goodwill." The value of the latter is a pressing concern for most business owners and investors.

This method of valuation helps confirm or improve on values established by the capitalization or leveraged cash flow methods.

To calculate business value using this method, the following variables are needed:

- Free cash flow
- Market value of tangible assets
- Safe rate of return
- Business RPM

Free cash flow, market value of tangible assets and RPM are developed as described earlier. A safe rate of return is the return on investment or "interest rate" one might receive from a highly liquid short-term investment. This is often two to three points less than Prime. A good example is the rate of interest offered on a short-term certificate of deposit.

With these variables in place value may be estimated using the following steps.

STEP 1: Determine Business Free Cash Flow.
This figure comes from the ERCON prepared to identify cash flow adjusted for management compensation.

Business Free Cash Flow = $19,932

STEP 2: Calculate a Return on Tangible Assets.
What could the investment in market value of tangible assets be earning if the money were invested elsewhere? To determine this, multiply their market value by the safe rate of return.

Recall from the earlier example, the market value of

assets included (for purposes of a business sale), the following assets: Real Estate @ $105,000, Inventory @ cost totaling $55,000, Furnishings, Fixtures and Equipment @ $5,000 Total $165,000.

$165,000 x 6.00% (safe rate of return) = $9,900 (return on tangible assets)

STEP 3: Determine the Business Excess Earnings.
Subtract the return on investment in tangible assets (see Step 2) from free cash flow.

$19,932 (free cash flow) - $9,900 (return on tangibles) = $10,032 (excess earnings)

STEP 4: Calculate Market Value of Business Excess Earnings .
This is the result of excess earnings multiplied by Business RPM.

$10,032 (excess earnings) x 2.57 (RPM) = $25,782 (value of excess earnings)

STEP 1: Determine Estimated Business Value.
Add the market value of business excess earnings to the market value of business tangible assets.

$165,000 (tangibles) + $25,782 (value of excess earnings) = $190,782 (business value)

Using the Excess Earnings Method

Use the excess earnings method to complement or confirm value determined by the capitalization method. Additionally, this method provides a good answer to a question many entrepreneurs ask: "How much is the goodwill worth?" Answering is easy because the formula automatically assigns a value to goodwill by identifying the income it creates. With this ability, it's easy to measure the growth of goodwill.　　Many buyers have discovered that business sellers often attempt to justify value by emphasizing how much more their business could be worth if certain initiatives were taken. A smart buyer will request predictions of investment required and income produced. Thereafter, the excess earnings can be used to predict changes in tangible asset values and free cash flow, and from there the "potential" business value is calculated. One quickly discovers the effort to create additional goodwill may not be as productive as envisioned. This is a good tool and technique for buyers dealing with sellers attempting to sell business potential instead of current or trailing earnings.

EXCESS EARNINGS VALUATION METHOD

Variables
| Free Cash Flow | $ 19,932 | Safe Rate 6.00% |
| Tangible Assets | $165,000 | RPM | 2.57 |

Business Free Cash Flow	$ 19,932
Tangible Assets	$ 165,000
Safe Rate of Return	6.00%
Return on Tangible Assets $9,900	<$ 9,900>
Business Excess Earnings	$ 10,032
Risk/Price Multiple	2.57
Value of Excess Earnings	$ 25,782
Value of Tangible Assets	$ 165,000
ESTIMATED BUSINESS VALUE	$ 190,782

　　Like its capitalization method cousin, the excess earnings method is a relatively simple calculation. Accuracy and reliability depends on variables developed and used.

Chapter 10
The Leveraged Cash Flow Method

The leveraged cash flow method sets the standard the business must match. The leveraged cash flow (LCF) method of valuation addresses two important goals of buyers, both of which are based on current market conditions: paying management compensation earnings and, paying off debt created to buy the business. The reason these goals dominate the process is that many entrepreneurs are buying themselves a job – a new lifestyle. These buyers do not always view a business acquisition as a dispassionate investment – their emphasis is on replacing income, not return on investment. In addition, most small businesses that sell will involve some type of acquisition financing. Buyers seek financial leverage to maximize the value of seed capital from savings used to become an entrepreneur. Owners who are sensitive to buyers' needs price their businesses accordingly and sell them much faster.

The leveraged cash flow method of valuation helps reveal what price the business can afford to support. It is an acid test standing in as a reality check. When the price doesn't make sense, just adjust the calculation to identify a more acceptable estimate. This is an important addition to an entrepreneur's negotiating skill because many businesses are overpriced. Often owners are so uncertain about how value is calculated, they establish a safeguard price that is far too high.

The LCF formula is flexible and versatile, too. It is constructed so variables are easily changed to examine different options. These may vary from market to market, business type to business type. This flexibility is needed when valuing small businesses because no two are alike. The LCF has been used to value businesses for as low as $5,000 and as high as $35 million and up. All with good accuracy by comparison with other more sophisticated approaches.

The Leveraged Cash Flow Method

The leveraged cash flow method of business valuation accommodates both sellers' desire for cash and buyers' need for terms. It includes the cost of acquisition financing as a determinant of value. Free cash flow is used to retire debt that is routinely secured. There are two primary sources of financing. One is a bank, which will offer more restrictive terms than the other – a seller. The variance in terms of financing will affect the cost or amount of financing available. This in turn affects the price in such a way that one type of financing typically produces a lower value than the other. Therefore, the cash flow method of valuation is presented in two forms: one with seller financing and the other using financing from a commercial lender. Together they help build a value range based on business cash flow. This range of values can be confirmed with the capitalization and excess earnings methods.

Seller Financing

There are many reasons owners are willing to finance businesses they sell. Financing from a bank is harder to secure, it takes longer, more disclosures are required and it's more expensive. By comparison, seller financing is a path of less resistance. It will make the opportunity more attractive, too. When the goal is to sell for the highest price, in the shortest time, for the least effort, seller financing is a big help. Compared to banks, sellers also have more faith in, and a willingness to accept, tangible and intangible assets as collateral for debt. They have direct experience with their ability to produce a financial result. Seller financing provides regular monthly income, perhaps for retirement following years of building a business. Finally, it may also make it possible for the seller to justify a higher price.

Interest Rates and Terms

Interest rates for sellers who finance their property can often be the same as those charged by a local lender. This is normally acceptable to buyers unless interest rates start to rise so high that the cost of financing dramatically affects the price. Just such a situation occurred in late 1970s and early 1980s when interest rates were as high as 20%. Business sellers took advantage of this opportunity by offering a much more desirable and lower rate.

Sometimes a seller will attempt to boost the sale price with substantial reductions in the interest rate charged on financing. IRS regulations set a floor on interest rate charged in an installment sale. IRS Code Sec. 24, 035 states, "Deferred payment sales where some or all of the payments are due more than one year after a sale and there is 'unstated' interest occurring after June 30, 1985 are subject to the imputed interest rate rules." The regulations continue to suggest "unstated interest" occurs when the rate charged is very low or zero. In these instances the IRS will treat the transaction as if a base rate of interest were charged that is greater than unstated interest collected. The effect of this treatment is a conversion of gross profit (from the sale of a business) that might have been more preferentially treated as a capital gain into ordinary income. The taxes due will be greater.

IRS Code Sec. 6532 indicates that where a transaction is found subject to the imputed interest rate rules, the applicable federal interest rate (AFR) will be used as a replacement rate.

The AFR is listed in the Tax Code, but for most purposes it is 9% on sales where deferred amounts collected does not exceed $2.8 million, and $6% on land sales between family members where the deferred amounts do not exceed $500,000. These rules are complex, however, and as with all other references to Tax Code provisions, seek advice from a qualified tax consultant.

The second financing variable to consider is the term. A general rule to guide determining this variable is "The life of the loan should be equal to or less than the service life of the asset securing the debt." Using this premise, a 10-year loan on an investment of videotapes for a video rental store might be inappropriate. Conversely, a three-year term for land with a new building is not long enough.

Businesses without real estate and including only personal property (furnishings, fixtures, equipment an inventory) are often financed for three, five or seven years. The difference is based on the business RPM, trailing and current earnings, cash flows, LTV, DCR and qualifications of the buyer.

Where real estate is used to secure the loan in addition business personal property, the financing term is normally 15, 20 or even 30 years. There may also be separate loans for the real estate and one or more categories of personal property. (See Chapter 16 "Special Situation" for a discussion of business valuation where no real estate is included, or where multiple loans are used to build value.)

Like its companion variable, interest rate, the longer the term the more financing available. However, one would not expect a seller to be positioned holding a 30-year loan on business real estate where obsolescence can easily occur. Most common are 15- to 20-year terms or the alternative of a 30-year amortization with a 15-year due date.

Using the Leveraged Cash Flow Method "LCF"

Four steps are needed to use the LCF method of valuing a business. The first is to simply retrieve free cash flow available from the ERCON performed in a due diligence. Be sure to use trailing earnings from the most current business fiscal year. If trends are strong use, a weighted value taken from three to five years past. Avoid using projected earnings since too many things can cause them to change. Also, the free cash selected will presume that an appropriate value for management compensation is considered.

In the second step, convert free cash flow into a stream of monthly payments. These will service the debt created. Divide the annual free cash flow by 12, since monthly payments are normally requested. In cases where bi-monthly, quarterly, semi-annual or annual payments are preferred, divide the free cash flow by 6, 4, 2, or 1 respectively.

Third, determine the amount of debt the free cash flow can support. (Recall the discussion of amortization as it pertains to financing.) The payment is identified in step two above. Next, the analyst will recommend a loan term, interest rate and future value at the due date of the loan (usually zero). From these four variables the loan amount is calculated. Using (or learning to use) an amortizing or financial calculator to determine loan variables is recommended.

The last step is to add equity to the loan amount – in this case a down payment that a capable buyer is willing to pay. This combination of equity and debt is business value. Here the valuation analyst's skill is crucial. (Market information is helpful.) As a rule of thumb consider the relationship of *down payment* to *management compensation* and the price paid for intangibles – *goodwill*. Consider the situation.

Determining Equity

Buyers who are buying a job tend to think of a business in these terms. They favorably view business opportunities whose downpayment is one to one and a half times annual management compensation. The former is a good benchmark for general use. In many cases business offerings request much more equity or downpayment. When surveying the market for common characteristics, pay less attention to what is offered. Focus on characteristics of businesses that are actually sold.

Equity may vary depending on the type or capital structure of a business, too. Small service companies with few assets and high profit margins can sell for a price equal to one year's management compensation. Very stable, asset-laden companies can command a premium, too. For them a downpayment can be twice management compensation or more. In cases where business trends are unfavorable and business RPM is low, equity required to buy can be less than one year's compensation.

In determining how much equity to input, a second consideration is goodwill. Business buyers hesitate when the price for intangible assets is more than one year's management compensation. They do not like to pay too much for this type of property unless it can be demonstrated that the assets are unique and direct drivers of revenue. Otherwise, a benchmark to follow is that equity should not exceed the annual management compensation. (This, too, will vary and often does when financing is shifted from the seller to a lender.)

Another way to determine down payment in the LCF method is based on fixing equity as a percent of value. To use this approach, assume the amount of equity that will be included. Subtract it, as a percent, from 1.00. The remainder is that percent of value representing debt. Divide the amount of financing or debt by this percent. The result is a business value. Subtract the financing and the difference is dollars of equity or down payment required.

Finally, it is possible to use business RPM (risk/price multipliers) to determine investor equity or the down payment portion of a business value. This technique will standardize the LCF method provided market forces are well known and reasonably stable. Comparison with other investments is possible. The amount of equity, expressed as a percent of management compensation, is calculated from the following table:

| Calculating Equity from Risk/Price Multiples | |
Business RPM	Equity
0.00 to1.00	0% to 50%
1.01 to 2.00	51% to 75%
2.01 to 3.00	76% to 100%
3.01 to 4.00	101% to 125%
4.01 to 5.00	126% to 150%

Using the table above if a risk/price multiple is between 0 and 1.00, the equity contributed to the investment (as a down payment) will be from zero to 50% of the annual management compensation up to $15,250. The XYZ Company, with a risk/price multiple of 2.57, indicates the range of equity will be from 76% to 100% of annual management compensation – from $22,875 to $30,500. Equity may be calculated as any amount within the range.

The RPM technique proves less helpful when market conditions are changing rapidly. Swift changes in demand for small business investments create equally swift and sometimes significant changes in business value.

LEVERAGED CASH FLOW METHOD
(Seller Financing)

VARIABLES:
Free Cash Flow $ 19,932   RPM   2.57
Tangible Assets $165,000   Mgt. Comp. $30,500

STEP 1: Calculate Monthly Payments for Debt.
Free Cash Flow $ 19,932.00
(x) Payments Per Period   12
Monthly Payments $ 1,661.00

STEP 2: Determine Amount of Financing.
Interest Rate   9.75%
Loan Term   15

Monthly Payment $ 1,661.00
Balance on Due Date $ 0
Serviceable Debt $156,792.00

STEP 3: Determine Business Value.
Affordable Loan Balance $156,792.00
(+) Equity (Mgt. Comp. * 1.00) $ 30,500.00
BUSINESS VALUE $187,292.00

Performing a Reality Check

Once the leveraged cash flow calculation is complete, move away from the details to inspect the overall result. Does the value calculated make good sense? There are four criteria to help entrepreneurs answer this question.

Realistic Financing. Review basic terms of financing to ensure they are consistent with reasonable expectations of the market. Examine length of loan, interest rate and amounts of payment in relationship to free cash flow available. If not, make final adjustments and recalculate.

Amount of Financial Leverage. The business value is the one that will attract the most investors willing to pay the price. Investors want financial leverage; opportunities offered that require more than 50% equity are considered less attractive.

Relationship of Equity to Management Compensation. When the down payment is greater than the annual compensation, the desirability of the investment is often reduced. As an average benchmark use a 1:1 ratio of equity to management compensation where both are equal. Higher ratios are possible with businesses that have an impressive track record of performance; those lower are not as reliable.

Relationship of Equity to Goodwill. With the exception of proven franchises, buyers are justifiably cautious about purchasing too much goodwill. Review the amount of intangibles in the business value. When this amount exceeds the equity, a good reason should be apparent. Otherwise, the opportunity loses luster.

Adjusting Variables

Many times a business value calculated can be improved with minor adjustments to variables. Here is when a conflict between the analyst's integrity and intellect occurs. A seller's desire to justify a higher price might prompt an increase in the term of financing or a reduction in the interest rate charged. It increases the amount of financing that a fixed amount of free cash flow can support to suggest the business can justify a higher price. Reducing the management compensation to increase free cash flow or raising the RPM have a similar effect. As expected, a buyer will do the opposite to reduce the investment indicated. Note the effect of the following adjustments:

Variable	Reduced	Increased
Interest Rate	Raises Value	Lowers Value
Loan Term	Lowers Value	Raises Value
Management Compensation	Raises Value	Lowers Value
Risk/Price Multiple	Lowers Value	Raises Value

For example, a seller can adjust the RPM to 4.5 very easily, since this is a subjective measure of performance. By also offering financing it is possible to lengthen the loan term to 20 years and reduce the interest rate to 9%. These adjustments produce the following results:

LEVERAGED CASH FLOW METHOD
(Seller Financing)

VARIABLES:
    Free Cash Flow $ 19,932   RPM   4.50
    Tangible Assets $165,000   Mgt. Comp. $30,500

STEP 1: Calculate Monthly Payments for Debt.
    Free Cash Flow $ 19,932.00
(x) Payments Per Period   12
    Monthly Payments $ 1,661.00

STEP 2: Determine Amount of Financing.
    Interest Rate   9.00%
    Loan Term   20
    Monthly Payment $ 1,661.00
    Balance on Due Date $ 0
    Serviceable Debt $184,612.00

STEP 3: Determine Business Value.
    Affordable Loan Balance $184,612.00
(+) Equity (Mgt. Comp. * 1.00) $ 45,750.00
    BUSINESS VALUE $230,362.00

The adjustments to loan term and interest rate increase business value by $43,070, or 23%. In the real world of business valuation, most businesses are offered with little regard given to justification of price. On those occasions where an owner has business valuation skill, it is clearly possible to manipulate the estimate of value to suit the purpose. A reality check will help reveal the validity of adjustments made. Challenge the value.

In the higher value terms of financing are more favorable than those previously offered. The equity appears attractive, too. At only 20% of business value, this creates financial leverage that will stimulate increased buyer interest. The amount of equity as a percent of management compensation, though, is less desirable. At 1.5 it could give buyers a reason to hesitate. Many will react by constructing their own RPM and justify a lower business value.

The biggest problem created by the adjustments lies in the relationship of price to goodwill. With tangible assets having a fair market value of $165,000, the value of goodwill is $65,434.58, or 2.15 times management compensation. This is very high and will be unappealing to many potential and qualified investors. Therefore, the adjusted business value, though possible, could be counterproductive and reduce the number of interested buyers. This does not support the goal of a business owner attempting to sell.

Make adjustments to the variables to refine business value and improve its accuracy. However, ensure that they remain consistent with actual marketplace conditions and the expectations of the principals involved.

Chapter 11
Cash Lowers the Price Not the Rewards

It is said that when valuing a business, develop a value range using the cost, market and income approaches. Combined, these are good indicators of value. When changes in financing occur, such as those illustrated in the latter part of the previous chapter, business values often change.

While most businesses that actually sell often involve some amount of seller financing, many do not. Indeed, Tax Code provisions (see Appendix B: Installment Sales) affecting the installment sale method of financing a business virtually assure seller financing will be less available than before. The alternative? Pay cash or seek financing elsewhere. As long as entrepreneurs believe in the benefits of financial leverage commercial lending institutions will remain a viable option.

The U.S. Small Business Administration (SBA) is a government established to assist entrepreneurs in most aspects of business start-up, expansion or acquisition. Small business valuation emphasizes financing and providing services to meet this need is at the core of the SBA's mission. Its activities are varied, however, and support entrepreneurs in other ways as well (e.g., through the Service Corps of Retired Executives – or SCORE – which includes more than 12,400 counselors in 389 chapters nationwide).

Business loans typically involve greater risk than real estate loans. This is because value is a derivative of tangible and intangible assets combined to create financial benefits. Both can evaporate fast. To encourage lenders to accept the greater risk of financing small businesses, the SBA offers, under certain conditions, guarantees of financing for small business entrepreneurs. Because these programs reduce risk to both borrower and lender, they increase a bank's willingness to make small business loans. When sellers want cash for a business, and buyers want to preserve financial leverage, commercial lenders get involved and when they get involved, so does the SBA.

SBA 7(A) Loan Guarantee Program

Under the terms and conditions of the 7(a) loan program, the SBA guarantees up to $750,000 of a private-sector loan: as much as 80% on loans of $100,000 or less, and 75% on loans of more than $100,000. A borrower may have more than one SBA loan at a time, as long as the total amount does not exceed the $750,000 cap. Loans may be made for a variety of reasons:

- To expand or renovate existing facilities
- To purchase equipment, inventory, fixtures or leaseholds
- To finance receivables and improve working capital
- To refinance existing debt if benefits to be realized by the borrower are compelling
- To provide lines of credit for businesses with seasonal variances
- To construct commercial buildings
- To purchase land or buildings for commercial use

Terms, Rates and Fees

There are no balloon payments, prepayment penalties, application fees or points permitted with an SBA loan. Payment plans may be tailored to the needs of the individual business and may be delayed for up to six months.

The length of time for repayment depends on the use of the proceeds and the ability of the borrower to repay. Most terms are as follows:

- Five to 10 years for working capital loans
- Up to 25 years for fixed assets, such as the purchase or major renovation of real estate or the purchase of equipment (not to exceed the useful life of the equipment)

Both fixed and variable interest rates are available. Rates are pegged at up to 2.25 percent over the lowest prime rate for loans with maturities of less than seven years, and up to 2.75 percent for seven years or more. For loans under $50,000, rates may be slightly higher. The prime rate is based on the lowest prime rate published in *The Wall Street Journal* on the day the SBA receives the application.

The SBA charges a guarantee fee. On loans with maturities of one year or less, the fee is 0.25% of the guaranteed portion of the loan. On loans with maturities of more than one year where the SBA's portion is $80,000, the guaranty fee is figured on an incremental scale between 3% and 3.875% of the guaranteed portion (75%). The fee equals 3% of the guaranteed portion up to $250,000: 3.5% of the next $250,000, and 3.875% of the remainder.

In addition to the guaranty fee charged at the time of disbursement, there is an ongoing fee of 0.5% of the balance of the loan. The lender (who is also permitted to charge a late fee of up to 5% of the payment amount for payments more than 10 days overdue) collects this fee monthly. An extraordinary servicing fee of up to 2% of the outstanding balance may be collected in cases involving construction or using accounts receivable or inventory for collateral. Application fees, commitment fees or prepayment fees are not permitted on term credits.

Collateral

Borrowers must pledge sufficient assets, to the extent that they are reasonably available, to adequately secure the loan requested. Personal guarantees are required from all the principal owners of a business – typically anyone with an ownership interest greater than 25%. Liens on principals' personal assets also may be required.

Eligibility

- To be eligible for a 7(a) loan, the business generally must be operated for profit, not be engaged in speculation investment, and fall within size standards the SBA sets. Loans cannot be made to businesses engaged in speculation or investment. The SBA determines if the business qualifies as a small business based on the average number of employees during the preceding 12 months or on sales averaged over the previous three years. Maximum size standards are as follows:
- Manufacturing – 500 to 1,500 employees
- Wholesaling – 100 employees
- Services – $2.5 million to $21.5 million in gross income
- Retailing – $5 million to $21 million in gross income
- General Construction – $13.5 million to $17 million in gross income
- Special Trade Construction – average annual gross income not exceeding $9 million
- Agriculture – $500,000 to $9 million in gross income

The SBA also considers the following important to a request for financing:

- Good character
- Management expertise and the commitment necessary for success
- Sufficient funds, including the SBA-guaranteed loan, to operate the business on a sound financial basis (management compensation and enough free cash flow to service debt)

- Feasible business plan
- Adequate equity or investment in the business
- Sufficient collateral
- Ability to repay the loan on time from the projected operating (free) cash flow

Certified/Preferred Lenders

Banks make SBA loans and the SBA guarantees them. The most active and expert participating lenders qualify for either the Certified Lenders Program or the Preferred Lenders Program. Both offer a quicker turnaround on loan applications (important when financing is tied to an acquisition timetable).

Certified lenders receive a partial delegation of authority (from the SBA) to approve loans and they hear a response on their loan guaranty applications within three days. Preferred lenders have full authority to approve loans and do not submit applications to the SBA. A list of participants in these loan programs is available through the local or regional SBA office.

Other Programs of Interest

Three other important features of the SBA are worthy of the entrepreneur's attention.

- Low Documentation (SBA *LowDoc*) loans are available to borrowers of $150,000 or less. The *LowDoc* features a one-page application, which reduces the paperwork burden for the borrower and the lender. Both complete the one-page guaranty application once lender requirements have been met. If the loan is approved, the SBA will guarantee 75% to 80% of the amount and provide a 36-hour turnaround to the lender. Businesses with average annual sales for the past three years not exceeding $5 million 100 or fewer employees, or business start-ups, are eligible for this program.
- SBA*Express* encourages lenders to make small loans to small businesses. Participating lenders use their documentation and procedures to approve, service and liqui-

date loans of up to $150,000. In return, the SBA guarantees up to 50% of each loan. SBA*Express* lenders can also offer revolving lines of credit to borrowers.

- SBA Prequalification is available to armed forces veterans, minorities, women, exporters, rural small business owners and business owners in certain specialized industries. This program enables the SBA to prequalify an applicant for a 7(a) loan guaranty before the applicant goes to the bank. The maximum loan amount is $250,000. SBA-designated intermediaries work with the applicant to strengthen the loan application, submit the request and, upon approval of the application, find an interested lender. *The application focuses on character, credit, experience and reliability rather than assets.*

Lender Versus Seller Financing

A key difference exists between lender versus seller financing when using the leveraged cash flow method of business valuation. With the latter the amount of financing is determined from loan terms and the amount of debt the business can *afford*. Typically 100% of free cash flow is committed to retire debt. Sellers are not so concerned about the relationship between debt and the market value of tangible assets serving as collateral.

Lender guidelines are more costly and challenging. These establish the upper limit of credit *available* to a small business borrower without regard to free cash flow. Debt is determined using loan-to-value and debt-coverage ratios, explained earlier in this text. When combined with other factors such as interest rate and terms on financing available, a bank lends less than a seller. In some cases, the amount of free cash flow committed to service debt is also less. When this happens the difference between free cash flow and annual debt service (ADS) on a bank loan may be diverted to pay off a smaller second mortgage to a seller. (Bankers often view the existence of such as a vote of confidence in the buyer from the seller. It can be an important incentive to lenders whose loan approval is wavering.)

To illustrate the immediate impact of bank lending guidelines on available financing, consider the following example.

- Loan-to-Value Ratio: 80% for all assets with an SBA Guaranty
- Debt-Coverage Ratio: 1.2
- Assets Market Value: $165,000
- Free Cash Flow: $19,932

With this information a maximum loan available can be determined. To do so, multiply the assets market value by the loan-to-value ratio.

$165,000 x 80% = $132,000 (maximum loan available)

Next, convert free cash flow into annual debt service when discounted by the bank's debt-coverage ratio. This is done as follows:

$19,932 ÷ 1.2 = $16,610 (annual debt service)

Divide the annual debt service figure by 12 to determine the monthly debt service. Apply the monthly payment (here $1,384.17) to the terms negotiated in order to calculate the loan amount affordable. Assume the interest rate is 9.75% and the loan term is 15 years. Here are the variables used with an amortizing calculator to determine the loan amount.

Payment	$ 1,384.17
Interest Rate	9.75%
Term	15
Future Value	0
Loan Amount	$130,660.00

Since the lender has set a debt ceiling of $132,000, the loan amount affordable ($130,660) should be acceptable. Notice, however, additional free cash flow still exists – the difference between business free cash flow and annual debt service on bank financing. In some cases, sellers refuse to accept any financing. When this occurs many often treat the excess free cash flow as added compensation to the buyer. A like amount is added to equity requirements. However, more frequently the excess free cash flow can pay the costs of a junior lien to a seller in those cases where the bank does not object. The amount of excess free cash flow is calculated as:

$19,932 - $16,610 = $3,322 (excess free cash flow)

Junior liens from sellers typically cost more. Their interest is higher and terms are shorter than senior liens by comparison. Assume the following conditions of a junior lien.

Payment	$ 276.83
Interest Rate	10.00%
Term	7
Future Value	0
Loan Amount	$16,675.00

Complete the leveraged cash flow valuation with bank financing option by combining both loans with a down payment. Use the same business RPM indicating a 1:1 ratio of equity to management compensation.

$130,660 (senior lien) + $16,675 (junior lien) + $30,500 (equity) = $177,835 (value)

The comparison to seller financing reveals the impact of a bank loan. Value is reduced by about five percent.

LCF/Seller Financing	$187,292
LCF/Bank Financing	<$177,835>
Difference	$ 9,457

The completed leveraged cash flow method using bank financing option follows.

LEVERAGED CASH FLOW METHOD
(Bank & Seller Financing)

VARIABLES:

Free Cash Flow	$ 19,932	RPM	2.57
Tangible Assets	$165,000	Mgt. Comp.	$30,500
DCR	1.2	LTV	80%

STEP 1: Calculate Monthly Payments for Debt.

Free Cash Flow	$19,932.00
(÷) Payments per period	12
Monthly Payments	$ 1,661.00

STEP 2: Determine Amount of Financing.

	1st Mortgage	2nd Mortgage
Interest Rate	9.75%	10.00%
Loan Term	15	7.00
Monthly Payment	$ 1,384.17	$ 276.83
Balance on Due Date	$ 0	$ 0
Serviceable Debt	$130,660.00	$ 16,675.00

STEP 3: Determine Business Value.

Total Financing Affordable	$147,335.00
(+) Equity (Mgt. Comp. * 1.00)	$ 30,500.00
BUSINESS VALUE	$177,835.00

Chapter 12
Building Confidence in Business Value

Imagine a contest where two archers compete by aiming at a target 200 feet away. Each gets four attempts to hit the bull's eye. The one judged most accurate will be the archer who places the most arrows closest to the center of the target.

The competition begins, and the first archer hits the bull's eye with one shot, next misses by an inch, then misses by two or three inches with the other two. Robin Hood would be proud. The second archer misses the bull's eye first by a half-inch, then twice by 12 to 15 inches and then the final arrow fails to hit the target at all. Based on these results the first archer is clearly more accurate. He had a better aim and produced a better result. One could have more confidence in the winner, especially if he were to act as a bodyguard.

Measuring business values and the confidence we can have in them is similar to an archery contest. If values created by the capitalization, excess earnings and both leveraged cash flow methods are all very similar, the accuracy is high. If, however, the spread of values is large, confidence in the final estimate will be less.

Measures of Central Tendency

"Central tendency" describes the general numeric location of a group of values. Three measures of central tendency exist: mean (M), median (MD) and mode (MO). The *mean* is the average of a group of values. The *median* is the value below and above which there are an equal number of values. The *mode* is the most frequently occurring value. In business valuation the mean and median can be used to help entrepreneurs measure confidence in the business value estimate. This technique involves several easy steps described in the following pages. Give this a try – the result is worth the effort.

Size of Value Range

Prior mention of a range of business values has been made on several occasions. Nowhere is the benefit of this range more apparent than when using it to measure the degree of accuracy or confidence entrepreneurs can place in value estimates. From earlier calculations, the business values for the example used are as follows:

Capitalization Method	$173,322
Excess Earnings Method	$190,782
Leveraged Cash Flow (Seller Financed)	$187,292
Leveraged Cash Flow (Bank Financed	$177,835

The range (R) of a set of values is the size of the spread –the distance between values at the upper and lower limits. It is calculated by subtracting the lowest business value (BV^l) from the highest business value (BV^H). This is accomplished with the following equation.

$$\$190{,}782 \ (BV^H) - \$173{,}322 \ (BV^l) = \$ \ 17{,}460 \ (R)$$

Next locate the median (MD) of the range of values. Remember, the median is the number appearing in the exact center, where half of all values in the range are above and half are below. The median is calculated by dividing the range in two. Thus:

$$\$17,460 \text{ (R)} \div 2 = \$8,730 \text{ (MD)}$$

Business Market Value

The business market value (MV) is the value entrepreneurs will consider the market price when buying, selling or trading a business. MV is a synthesis of all values in the range. This may include those suggested for calculation in this text and any others the entrepreneur chooses to use. MV is the value that exists exactly in the center of the value range – the bull's eye. Because the base of the range is not zero, the median value (of the range) is added to the lowest value in the range to establish MV.

$$\$173,322 \text{ (BV}^{1}) + \$8,730 \text{ (MD)} = \$182,052 \text{ (MV)}$$

Variance between Mean and Market Values

Here is the first opportunity to test the accuracy of the values. To begin, calculate the mean of the values in the range. This is easily accomplished: Add all values and divide the sum by the number of values added. The result then is the mean business value (M) or average of all values in the range.

Capitalization Method	$173,322
Excess Earnings Method	$190,782
Leveraged Cash Flow (Seller Financed)	$187,292
Leveraged Cash Flow (Bank Financed)	<u>$177,835</u>
Total	$729,231

$$\$729,231 \div 4 = \$182,308 \text{ (M)}$$

Notice there is a small variance (**V**) between market ($182,052) and mean ($182,308) business values. Calculate this by subtracting the smaller from the larger. It does not matter which is larger since this is a measurement of size. Also, this approach is easier since it does not result in a negative value.

$$\$182,308 \text{ (M)} - \$182,052 \text{ (MV)} = \$256 \text{ (V)}$$

This variance is created because business values calculated are not spread evenly across the range. If three values were clustered at the low or high end of the range, the variance of the mean to the median would be larger. A wider variance could also occur if three values were similar and one was very different. The effect of a broader spread of values on a confidence index will be illustrated later.

Confidence in Value

Remember, like in the archery contest, less variance from the bull's eye means greater accuracy and more confidence in the result. The confidence index attempts to measure this variance. To proceed, follow the next simple steps.

First, divide the variance (V) between mean and market business values by the median of the range. In this case one using only those values within the range – not much larger value estimates. The answer is expressed as a percent of variance (V%).

$$\$256 \text{ (V)} \div \$8,730 \text{ (MD)} = .029 \text{ (V\%)}$$

Next convert V% to a percent (2.9%) and subtract it from 100%. The answer is 97.1%. To the entrepreneur, this means all values *in the value range* are within 97.1 percent of the market value indicated. Following this line of logic, one would conclude the accuracy of the business market value estimate and confidence one can place in this figure are high.

Confidence Index Calculation

STEP 1: Calculate the Mean of Values.

Total of Values	$729,231
(÷) No. of Values	4
Mean (M)	$182,308

STEP 2: Calculate the Range.

BV^H	$190,782
(-) BV^L	$173,322
Range	$ 17,460

STEP 3: Calculate the Median of the Range.

Range	$ 17,460
(÷) One-Half the Range	2
Median (MD)	$ 8,730

STEP 4: Calculate Market Value.

Median (MD)	$ 8,730
(+) BV^L	$173,322
Market Value	$182,052

STEP 5: Calculate the Variance.

Mean (M)	$182,308
(-) Market Value	$182,052
Variance	$ 256

STEP 6: Convert Variance to Percent Variance.

Variance	$ 256
(÷) Median (MD)	$ 8,730
Percent of Variance	.029

STEP 7: Calculate Confidence Index.

Percents Available	1.00
(-) Percent of Variance	.029
CONFIDENCE INDEX	.971

When the Spread is Large

Recall the chapter on leveraged cash flow valuations using seller financing. To justify a higher value, a seller adjusted the variables. The interest rate was reduced, the term of financing was extended, the RPM was raised and the resulting business value calculated was $230,362. Suppose this value were used in the range instead of $187,292. Accuracy is affected and the Confidence Index falls to 69%. The calculation process follows:

Confidence Index Calculation

STEP 1: Calculate the Mean of Values.

Total of Values	$772,301
(÷) No. of Values	4
Mean (M)	$201,842

STEP 2: Calculate the Range.

BV^H	$230,362
(-) BV^L	$173,322
Range	$ 57,040

STEP 3: Calculate the Median of the Range.

Range	$ 57,040
(÷) One-Half the Range	2
Median (MD)	$ 28,520

STEP 4: Calculate Market Value.

Median (MD)	$ 28,520
(+) BV^L	$173,322
Market Value	$193,075

STEP 5: Calculate The Variance.

Mean (M)	$201,842
(-) Market Value	$193,075
Variance	$ 8,767

STEP 6: Convert Variance to Percent Variance.

Variance	$ 8,767
(÷) Median (MD)	$ 28,520
Percent of Variance	.31

STEP 7: Calculate Confidence Index.

Percents Available	1.00
(-) Percent of Variance	.31
CONFIDENCE INDEX	.69

Chapter 13
Buy – Price as Power

Limited knowledge of business value is a hindrance to negotiations. Sellers may overprice businesses offered for sale. Informed buyers easily offend them when responding with legitimate counterproposals. Sellers forget their price may have been a fastball, high and outside. The only result of this all too frequent and brief exchange is the principals stop talking – an opportunity to advance is lost.

Business valuation skill empowers buyers, sellers and the acquisition process. Core issues are confronted head on. When both parties understand how business value is calculated, it is easier to close the gap between buyer and seller positions, but the high-spirited competition and negotiations can remain lively and fair. And the final outcome is a win-win transaction.

The often-quoted statistic that four out of five business start-ups fail means an equal number of owners fail, too. Their errors begin before a business is acquired. By addressing certain essentials, however, the potential for success improves.

- Understand non-negotiables.
- Know what a target property is worth.
- Communicate value to encourage acceptance.

Non-Negotiables

Buyers must know their capabilities. It is unwise to have unrealistic expectations. Moreover, recognizing critical factors of success helps prevent trouble before it begins. Observing non-negotiables are one way this is accomplished. Non-negotiables are things the entrepreneur cannot do without. To do so makes failure a near certainty. Following are three non-negotiables entrepreneurs should add to their list.

Non-Negotiable #1: "Don't pay too much."

Entrepreneurs who start, buy or exchange into a business make this their mantra for life. It is never knowingly violated. When it is, the path to poor results is already underfoot. After learning effective valuation techniques, how could this occur? Adrenaline is powerful. When a live business candidate emerges, the rush of excitement is persuasive enough to overpower reason. It's easy for the heart to overrule the head. Business valuation techniques help restore a healthy balance and prevent mistakes.

Non-Negotiable #2: "Seek the creative fulfillment from entrepreneurship."

Many entrepreneurs forget to consider an important issue when acquiring a business: Business owners do well and do best what they like most. They have to, because entrepreneurs must be willing to work 16 hours a day for themselves instead of eight hours for someone else.

Remember John Wayne's famous role as J.B. Books in *The Shootist*? The Duke plays a rough sheriff in the Old West who, at the end of his days, has established a considerable reputation for himself. Ron Howard, playing a young and impressionable admirer, asks Books what's caused him to be so great. The reply, (paraphrased here) was classic wisdom for the American entrepreneur: "Well, it isn't because I'm so quick on the draw, because others are faster. And it's not because I can shoot so straight, because others are more accurate. I suppose it's because when it comes time to shoot, most men hesitate, just for a second, and that's all the advantage I need. I'm willing to pull the trigger."

Entrepreneurs are willing to act. The lure of entrepreneurship is strong because when engaged in creative activity we are closest to our inner source. We become what we create. When successful, we are validated. A new sense of self-worth and confidence emerges.

Non-Negotiable #3: "Financial autonomy is the goal."

Business is the business of the American system of free enterprise. Business ownership is the mechanism entrepreneurs choose to accomplish their goals. Performance leads to profit. Profit leads to choice. Choices lead to freedom. In this quest, business valuation skills offer a useful tool.

Target Property Value

There are many businesses available for purchase. Some are good opportunities – others are one of the four out of five heading for failure. There must be a compelling reason to acquire a business whose trend of trailing revenue and earnings is declining. Instead, find the business that is thriving, surviving or can be reenergized by identifying and scaling a growth wall in the path of progress. Financial autonomy has a better chance of occurring when a business shows a favorable track record.

Good business opportunities are often overpriced. Sifting through all the opportunities, both good and bad, to find the best value is the goal. But this can be time-consuming, and entrepreneurs are pressed for time. So, the objective of smart buyers is to know what information to ask for, and to ask for it early.

First Impressions

Buyers cannot construct an offer involving a commitment of financial resources without knowing what benefits and income go with the property. That is like buying a property "sight unseen," and it's unwise. Buyers should not be expected to make offers based on innuendo, business potential and the romance of ownership. They are well advised and rewarded when their focus remains fixed on the economic rewards available.

Conversely, sellers can't be expected to open the books to every buyer expressing a casual interest. Serious intent should be demonstrated. Otherwise requests for financial disclosures are met with resistance and rightly so – buyers could be competitors in disguise, attempting to pick the seller's pockets for competitive intelligence. Requests for an executed non-disclosure agreement may be premature, however. The trick is to find out if both buyer and seller are in the same ballpark.

Consider the power of first impressions. With people they can be revealing and accurate. In fact, everything afterward is an attempt to confirm what is already intuitively known. Business opportunities are similar. It isn't necessary to perform a due diligence to develop a quick opinion of business value. Using three valuation strategies, a few variables help form a reasonably accurate first impression.

Price

When businesses are offered for sale, a price is often announced. This is a seller's opening statement of business value – and never to be accepted blindly. Occasionally a business is available but no price is stated. This is typically the result of a seller who 1) doesn't know the value of the property, 2) hopes to find a buyer who doesn't know the value of their property either, or 3) has a high standard of confidentiality. In either case it is difficult to proceed far, since financial disclosures will be equally limited. Don't invest too much time.

Terms

Generally speaking, the word "terms" means financing and its conditions. For reasons described earlier, financing provided by a seller is more attractive to most buyers. Where seller financing is not available, the buyer needs a good knowledge of loan criteria from potential commercial lenders. Investment leverage in business acquisitions can improve their financial return. It will be important to consider the cost to service debt from business cash flow. This is something else a buyer needs to know early.

Assets

There are many reasons to ask about the market value of assets. To begin, this will reveal the type of property for sale and the value of assets within each category. It will permit a buyer to calculate the portion of the asking price representing goodwill. It identifies the amount of collateral available to secure financing from a bank. It puts a seller on the defensive by challenging the asking price of property being sold. Curiously, when buyers ask the simple question, "What do I get for my money if I buy this business?" sellers often choke. That can be a revealing response. The better answer is "Income, assets and a marketing opportunity."

Revenue, EBIT and Cash Flow

A request for details like revenue, EBIT and cash flow threaten a seller more than broad-based inquiries. Knowing business revenue, however, is about as broad as it can get and shouldn't create unfavorable exposure. More importantly, getting revenue opens the door to inquire about trailing revenue that reveals business trends, which is important to the valuation process.

EBIT (earnings before income taxes) is a little more difficult to secure. Remember, sellers maximize expenses to minimize taxable earnings. Recognize also sellers understand this because they are doing it. Their problem is they may not be able to articulate it confidently, or precisely, to buyers. Position a request for EBIT as a request for business earnings before taxes. Link it to an understanding there is a difference between taxable income and cash flow. Everybody knows that in business it's not what the business earns that counts – it's what ownership gets to keep. That information is more private.

The stage is set to get an "estimate" of business cash flow. It may be helpful to point out the benefit of receiving limited information. It helps advance the inquiry by creating added interest. Every seller wants to create more interest. Recall the shortcut offered in Chapter 3 that described how entrepreneurs quickly size up a business. Add a request for monthly cash expenses, and if received, estimate the business's cash flow.

Management Compensation

Most buyers know how much income from employment they need to support their lifestyle. It is always helpful to know how much existing ownership believes management compensation should be. This is not a threatening request. Compare answers to the employment income tables in Chapter 4. They can confirm estimates made and provide the basis to challenge them.

Capitalization

Buyers who accept a business asking price leave sellers to do their thinking for them. This is a lazy, dangerous approach and so easy to avoid with the right skill. It pays to be a skeptic. Buyers demonstrate a healthy sense of skepticism by challenging representations made, such as the asking price. This is the easiest and most obvious way to negotiate a lower sales price. The reason more buyers don't take this approach, though, is because they are unable to use valuation techniques to justify a different position – they have nothing to argue with. For this reason, business valuation becomes a powerful tool.

The simplest way to challenge an asking price is by subjecting it to a capitalization method of determining business value. Assume the following from the example of the XYZ Company used in previous chapters:

- Asking price: $300,000
- Terms: 25% equity with seller financing for 15 years at 10% ($2,417.86 monthly)
- Market value of tangible assets: $165,000
- Revenue: $608,951 EBIT: $20,920 Cash Flow: $50,442
- Management compensation: $30,500
- Capitalization rate: 11.5%

From research and market knowledge the investor knows management compensation should be $30,500 and capitalization rates are 11.5%.

Begin the price challenge by using variables provided by the seller – price and cash flow – to figure the rate of return. Free cash flow is $19,932 (cash flow of $50,432 minus $30,500 management compensation). The equation to determine the rate of return becomes:

$$\$19,932 \div \$300,000 = \underline{.0664} \text{ or } 6.64\% \text{ (rate of return)}$$

At the asking price of $300,000 the rate of return to an investor is 6.64%. However, this is less than the expected capitalization rate of 11.5%. At the asking price, the business does not offer a competitive rate of return.

Now, calculate the amount of income that should be available from an investment of $300,000 producing the expected rate of return. Substitute an 11.5% capitalization rate and recalculate:

.115 (11.5%) x $300,000 = $34,500 (free cash flow)

To produce the desired capitalization rate, the income (free cash flow) should be $34,500. The actual amount is $19,932 or 42% less, based on market indicators of performance. This is another indication the business is overpriced.

Finally, calculate the adjusted current business value by using current free cash flow and the expected capitalization rate:

$19,932 ÷.115 (11.5%) = $173,322 (adjusted sales value)

Based on these criteria, a buyer can determine the business is overpriced by roughly $125,000. The analysis is fast, easy and revealing. Wide discrepancies in asking price and value are commonplace. With this information the buyer now can terminate the inquiry or, if the only apparent problem with the business is the price, attempt to negotiate it lower.

Another productive approach is to ask the seller to explain how the price of $300,000 was constructed. This yields valuable information. Or request additional information to shed new light on the issue. In the absence of meaningful evidence or willingness to listen to reason, don't waste too much time. Move on.

Excess Earnings

A second way to challenge the asking price is by applying the excess earnings method to confirm a business asking price. A business RPM (risk/price multiple) is needed. This is difficult to do without the benefit of a due diligence. Circumvent the process (early in the inquiry) by interviewing the seller. Explain how an RPM is created (See Chapter 6). Let sellers assign values needed. Note, these can be challenged later if a due diligence indicates a need for adjustments.

If a seller is unwilling to provide this assistance, the buyer can make a general estimate of the values leading to an RPM. Bear in mind, however, this means a seller is showing an unwillingness to even talk about the business they want to sell. Their motivation may not be very high.

Begin with variables known or those that can be calculated from what is given. Free cash flow is $19,932 and market value of tangible assets is $165,000. First calculate the value of excess earnings:

$300,000 - $165,000 = <u>$135,000</u> (value of excess earnings)

The asking price thus includes $135,000 for excess earnings or goodwill. Next calculate the RPM needed to support this investment. Recall, excess earnings are the same as free cash flow.

$135,000 ÷ $19,932 = <u>6.77</u> (risk/price multiple)

A 6.77 business RPM is off the scale that measures small business performance. It could only occur in a very hot seller's market or when a business has almost no margin for error or risk. With the exception of some dot.com businesses this type of seller's market seldom occurs. And few businesses, if any, are so devoid of investment uncertainty. At this point the buyer can terminate the analysis or, as before, indicate the need for evidence to support use of such a high business RPM.

Leveraged Cash Flow

Leveraged cash flow is the acid test of business value. Other measures of value are good, but this challenge measures the investor's ability to afford the price. It is very telling. To complete this challenge one must know the cash flow and cost of debt service, which, as offered, is $2,417.86 per month or $29,014 per year. Calculate management compensation:

$50,432 - $29,014 = <u>$21,418</u> (cash flow for management compensation)

Perform a reality check. Financial leverage is good, since the seller offers the business for 25% down ($75,000). Management compensation is deficient to expectations by $9,082, or 29%. This is a problem because it may not enable buyers to support a reasonable lifestyle. The relationship of equity ($75,000) to management compensation ($21,418) of 3.5 to 1 is also out of balance when compared to small business benchmarks. Finally, the goodwill at $135,000 is 1.8 times equity required and 6.3 times management compensation. This business price is too high for expectations.

Reversing roles is the easiest way to convey the desirability of the seller's asking price. Ask if he or she would feel comfortable with the business price, amount of goodwill, terms of finance and management compensation offered by the proposed acquisition. Ask if he or she thinks other buyers will show strong interest – or if any already have. Attempt to move the seller to a position that reveals flexibility. If possible, proceed to the next step, illustrating what price does make sense. If the seller remains inflexible, stop the inquiry. There is little chance of converting this situation into an attractive opportunity.

To calculate the best price using the leveraged cash flow approach, return to the previous equation and subtract management compensation from cash flow. The remainder is free cash flow that can be used to service debt. This substitution of management compensation for debt service ensures that the buyers personal service income needs can be met. Next, divide free cash flow by the number of payments made per year (12) on financing. This is the monthly payment available to service debt. Then recalculate the present value of the debt using the monthly payment. This reveals the amount of financing the business can afford to pay. Finally, in the absence of a business RPM to calculate a downpayment, use a common benchmark to determine this amount – one year's management compensation.

Notice use of a 10% interest rate on financing (as proposed) instead of a lower 9.75% market rate. This appears to be a compromise to the seller, but it actually advances the buyer's cause by reducing the amount of financing, and therefore, the price.

Leveraged Cash Flow Challenge

STEP 1:	Cash Flow	$ 50,432.00
	Management Compensation	<$ 30,500.00>
	Cash Flow for Mgmt. Comp.	$ 19,932.00
STEP 2:	Free Cash Flow	$ 19,932.00
	Periods Per Year	12
	Periodic Payments Available	$ 1,661.00
STEP 3:	Term	15 years
	Rate	10.00%
	Payment	$ 1,661.79
	Future Value	$ 0
	Loan Amount	$154,568.41
STEP 4:	Loan Amount	$154,568.41
	Equity (Down Payment)	$ 30,500.00
	BUSINESS VALUE	$185,068.41

Notice the value indicated is $2,223.59 less than the value calculated earlier ($187,292) using the LCF method. The variance is created by a slightly higher interest rate on financing. A formidable challenge can be presented to ownership's offering price of $300,000.

The Right Price

The shrewdest investors follow the simplest approach. They identify the price at which the business value meets their expectations. They communicate their position clearly and firmly. Then they stick to their value and negotiate things that don't matter. And they never bluff.

In each case the result is the same. Profit is earned the day ownership is transferred.

Entrepreneurs following these strategies know they do not need to buy every business to be successful. It is only important to invest in good values. A business purchased for the right price can produce enough profit to compensate entrepreneurs for months or a year's worth of earnings. It is worth waiting for. A bad deal can be equally costly and is worse than no deal at all.

Chapter 14
Sell – Prepare and Negotiate From Strength

All business sellers want the highest price in the shortest time for the least effort. Preparing the business for sale is the best way to accomplish these objectives. And this should begin at least a year before the business is offered for sale.

History indicates that uncertainty about business value

often drives up prices. This is a reaction to the fear of selling for too little. Leaving "room to negotiate" is not an unreasonable tactic until the room becomes the size of a gymnasium. Then this frequent justification becomes thin. It will not stand up against the sound logic of a well-conceived business valuation presented by a buyer.

Overpricing a property discourages buyers from pursuing an inquiry beyond the initial phase. With fewer buyers in tow, options are limited. The consequence is a limitation on the ability to negotiate from strength, sellers are easily placed on the defensive, and the outcome can be a sale of the business below market.

Basic Goals

To avoid selling too low successful sellers and brokers prepare to deal with the expected and unexpected aspects of selling a business. It can be a complex process. With good preparation, however, it is possible to achieve good results. They follow a seven-step plan to sell a business.

1) Give the buyer what they want.
2) Improve the buyer's financial condition.
3) Do things for buyers they cannot do for themselves.
4) It's easier to keep a buyer than find a new one.
5) Focus on what works.
6) Find ways to increase the supply of buyers.
7) Use the principle of attraction.

Successful sellers adopt a buyer's perspective to anticipate their moves. In other words, they do their thinking early to ensure better execution later.

To begin, examine what a seller's needs.

Highest Price

In the beginning, a business's highest price is one that will attract the greatest number of buyers. The ability to create a recognizable value is paramount. Try to imagine how much easier it is to negotiate potentially lucrative finer points of one deal when three more are in play. In the end, the highest price of a business is the value one buyer is ready, willing and able to pay – today.

One may infer the highest price has the potential to create a sale in the shortest amount of time. In most cases this will be true. Knowing what the highest price is then is a more important issue to sellers planning to market their business. Time is money. While a business is on the market, interest and other related holding costs continue. There are other direct and indirect costs, too, which can have equal or greater impact.

Shortest Time

When most entrepreneurs decide to sell, they want it to happen yesterday. This is because a new business vision, inconsistent with current conditions, may already be in place in their mind. Under these conditions ownership's focus is distracted and their effectiveness as management is diminished. This is a bad combination of events and can be costly. Standards of performance decline, and new opportunities are missed. The entrepreneurial spirit that drove the company to success is diminished. Burnout can easily occur.

When a property is available for a long time (more than six months), the owner can also become frustrated with the sales process. This is natural and easier to deal with when one knows what to expect. Frustration is greater if ownership's intent to sell does not remain confidential. Employees are not blind. Learning the boss is selling out may encourage them to consider other employment. In a time when the country is experiencing a labor shortage, this can be very costly. New employees must be found and trained before becoming productive – another distraction. Customers learning of the business sale may notice changes, too, and take their business elsewhere. When attempting to sell, the timing of these reactions could not be worse.

The combination of factors described can negatively affect revenue, expenses, EBIT, cash flow and the business value. Worse, intelligent buyers noticing a business languish on the market will take longer to act, hoping the price will fall more. Clearly the situation can be grim for the unprepared. There is, however, a solution.

Working behind the scenes, sellers can anticipate and develop a complete business disposition strategy. It takes six months, a year or perhaps even two if results are to be maximized. But it is worth the effort.

Least Effort

Face it. Selling a business is not always easy. It is not wise to assume the one-in-a-million buyers with money to burn will magically appear. It is better to prepare for the typical buyer. With a good plan, the preparation to sell, and the sales process, can be done in small increments over time to reduce the effort by a considerable degree. Eventually work adds up. In this way, a little effort here and there becomes the strategy that works best.

Time on the market is correlated to preparation. When a business offering is well planned and available at a reasonable price, a sale occurs much faster. That is because capable buyers know a good deal when they see one. They also know it won't last. A good sales plan and pricing strategy gives buyers a sense of urgency to take action sooner, while they still can. Building a sense of urgency among buyers makes the seller's job easier.

The importance of planning a sales strategy is clearly illustrated by the problem-solving training NASA astronauts receive. For example, when confronted with only 10 minutes of remaining air in space, what should they do? The correct answer is develop and think through all the options for nine minutes and execute the best in the last minute. As with most successful ventures, the effort required is 90% preparation and 10% percent perspiration.

Factors presented in the following discussion illustrate how a business can be prepared for sale. Using a diligent approach, an exciting offering can be made. Buyers will take the ball and run afterward. The seller's work from the first day on the market to closing will seem effortless. That is the goal.

Business Location

As with commercial real estate, a business's location is relatively fixed. This is almost certain when a business owns the real estate it occupies. It is likely also true where the location is leased. Only in the dot.com world has this changed.

Location is an important driver of customer traffic and revenue for many businesses. As long as this remains true, location will have a major effect on business value. When preparing a business for sale, it is not important to find ways the location can be improved. It is more important to develop assurances that the location will not change. So to prepare the location for sale, sellers work to assure buyers continued occupancy in the existing business location(s) is secure.

Ensure Continued Occupancy

There are several things sellers can do to improve their position with respect to a location. If leased, renegotiating the terms is a good place to start. An extension of the current lease term with options to renew for additional terms will be appealing to a buyer. Keep in mind, the objective is to ensure the potential term of occupancy should be greater than the term of any financing secured to acquire the business. At the time of lease renegotiation, it may also be advisable to lock in periodic increases in the rent and other terms of the lease. This will be particularly true if the location is highly desirable. Terms negotiated do not need to take effect until the business is sold.

If the real estate is owned by the business ownership, now may be a good time to refinance the property and withdraw equity. This is for two reasons. First, it is apparent a transition is about to occur. Increasing cash reserves can be helpful to the process. Second, if the buyer of the business acquires the real estate, too, financing is already in place. One factor that may affect a refinance option could be the seller's anticipated use of the installment sale method to sell the business and real estate. In most cases the debt would have to be paid for this to occur. Another is when market conditions indicate rental rates for the type of property leased are not high enough to allow monthly rent to service monthly payments on the debt created by refinancing the building. (For more on the status of a business with or without real estate see Chapter 16, Special Situations – Separate the Business from the Real Estate.)

Develop a Web Address

Website development is another form of location. It is said businesses not participating in e-commerce will not be in business within a few years. While there are surely many businesses prospering from Internet locations the world can visit, the ability to deliver a hamburger and fries is still a long way off. Until that time cyberspace does not replace the conventional bricks and mortar of a physical location. Nevertheless, creation of a location on the Web does have promotional value. It can attract more inquiries to a business. And when offered for sale, it is among the first places a buyer will visit to see what the business looks like. That is an important argument for the development of a Website prior to the sale of a business.

Business Condition

Many things can be done to improve the condition of a business property before it is offered for sale. Some just maintain value, while others have the potential to create improvement. Contrast the experience of selling a business to selling a home. To improve curb appeal, sellers trim the bushes, mow the lawn, add landscaping, freshen the paint, make repairs and clean the place up in general. It looks nicer, indicating good care and fewer problems. As a result it is easier to justify the asking price.

The same strategy works with a business. By all means clean up and fix up the place. Sell off dated or undesirable inventory if it exists. Attend to repairs needed in equipment. Release nonessential employees and replace them by outsourcing if possible. All these things will help the business look attractive when a buyer visits.

When considering ways to improve the condition of the

property for a sale don't forget about the intangible assets, either. Many deserve attention which, if given, have the potential to justify – even increase – business value. In fact, some sellers prepare their business for sale so well they decide to keep it after all. In either case, the cost/benefit relationship of this effort is bound to be favorable. Here are other considerations in anticipation of a business sale.

Reduce Uncertainty

Most sellers want to advertise the sale of their business to everyone and keep it a secret. Clearly, this is hard to do because confidentiality is easily lost. Overcome this potential liability by diffusing the negative effects of a leak that the business is for sale. It is best to ask oneself, "Who does it matter to, and how will it affect them?" Since employees and customers are most likely to be affected, and their unfavorable reactions could cause the most problems, they should be considered first. The goal is to reduce the impact of an impending sale on their attitude to zero.

Entrepreneurs reduce the uncertainty of a pending sale very simply: Periodically state or remind people every business asset owned is for sale every day it is owned. This candid expression of an entrepreneur's style builds trust by removing uncertainty. People pay less attention and are not as affected by rumors. They got used to the idea early.

A second way to reduce uncertainty is by preparing in private as mentioned earlier. The longer associates live with the knowledge that a change of ownership may be coming, the more time they have to consider their options. It has been shown advance preparations shorten the marketing time for a business with an attractive price. By squeezing the marketing cycle from both ends – keeping intent private and setting the stage for a fast sale – there is less time to lose key people.

A third way to reduce uncertainty for buyers is to stop skimming. Recall, skimming is income received but not reported for income tax purposes. Recall also it is that part of the business price the seller receives before selling the business. Very importantly, recall it is illegal. Recover business value and eliminate tax and legal entanglements by reporting all income. To be an effective driver of value, skimming should cease at least one year prior to the time a business is offered for sale. In this way all revenue can be included in the record of trailing business financial results.

In similar fashion, and at the same time, it is advisable to reduce the number and amount of perks enjoyed by owner-ship. Results reported change. Removing these benefits lowers operating costs. EBIT and cash flow increase. Even though an earnings reconstruction can demonstrate actual business earn-ing power, it is better to keep the process uncomplicated. Buyers will have more confidence and can take action sooner.

Training is another area of concern to buyers. They are often unsure of their ability to run the business as successfully as current ownership. This is natural. Business sales often include a certain amount of training for a new owner. This helps ensure a smooth transition. Training will be especially important if management needs specific operating skills. Anticipate a buyer's need for training by defining how it could occur and what it should include. This is normally done one of two ways.

- If a business is a franchise, a training program provided by the franchiser is an excellent resource. The buyer's attendance will probably be required before taking over. Arrangements to secure training from franchise corpora-tions will vary, but most will be cooperative and enthusi-astic about helping.

- Working side by side with the buyer in all phases of busi-ness operations is a second approach to training.

To ensure the quality of time spent for both, outline a brief curriculum to follow. It may be modeled after the basic com-ponents of a business: finance; control; marketing; sales; pro-duction; and service. What does the buyer need to know about each? In addition, build a timetable covering the basics and show how a seller's involvement with the business will gradually decrease. It need not last more than 60 days in many cases. This is important, too, because buyers normally want to take control as soon as possible. Sellers still in the business may not agree with decisions of the new controlling authority. They can disagree and this is not complementary to the work at hand.

A final word about training buyers. In most cases they will provide for some type of training in the buy/sell agreement. If the sale is for cash or 100% percent exchanges, training is not so important. If, however, an installment sale method is used, a thoroughly trained buyer is crucial. It is their skill and ability to manage the business successfully that ensures the installment payments due to the seller are made.

Increase Business Visibility

Greater name and brand awareness of a business in the year prior to a sale offers many benefits. Increased revenue and a larger target market of potential buyers are two worthy of a seller's attention. It is possible to increase them by instituting basic principles of marketing, advertising and public relations.

Ensure that marketing themes and appeals are attractive to a target clientele. This is the equivalent of painting the house. Keep company themes and slogans in all marketing materials and on stationery. It may be necessary to build a company brochure to create the perception of an established presence in the market. Consider hiring a marketing consultant to make sure the business has a good message that is well received.

Increase advertising. Advertising dollars properly spent in the year preceding a sale may draw the attention of the largest customer of all – a buyer for the business. Work to create the impression that the doors are wide open and the business is filled with customers. Remember, the real intent of advertising is to attract inquiries. With more inquiries, more sales occur.

Become a local expert. Many do not fully understand the business of public relations. They think delivering press releases to local news organizations (to be printed for free) is the objective. While basically true, this approach needs refinement.

Before attempting public relations initiatives, consider the editors' position. Each day they must manufacture news from current events. They never have enough material to fill all the print space or air time available. They are always looking for more material that is relevant and meaningful. Press releases that present new information about the community, how events affect groups of people, or interesting professional trends attract their attention. Sellers who can provide this information receive a printed credit for the effort. That seems like a little but it is very valuable.

An identifying credit as the source elevates the seller to expert status. Taken a step further, by offering nonsensitive business information sellers can become a regular source for news and reactions to other events. Companies who do this best are those that differentiate themselves well from competitors. Their differences, when clearly defined, become their strengths.

Try to make contact with news organizations quarterly during the year prior to a sale. If only one news release is used, it can still be influential when shown to a buyer. And finally, there is an old saying that goes, "Any press is good press." Don't believe this when preparing a business for sale. Bad press is not good and damages the seller's goal of achieving the highest price, in the shortest time, with the least effort.

Conduct a Due Diligence

Political candidates have themselves investigated prior to a run for office. This provides an opportunity to see themselves through the eyes of a voter. Afterward they are in a better position to give voters what they want.

Sellers can anticipate a buyer's reaction to their business by performing a due diligence prior to a sale. Hiring a business valuation consultant is a good way to do this, but they are far and few between. Material in this book is intended to help readers do it themselves. There are three objectives to consider.

First, identify the business strengths and weaknesses. This helps guide the effort to reinforce problem areas. It also points out benefits sellers sometimes do not see, which can be emphasized in a sales marketing plan.

Second, performing a due diligence improves objectivity and expectations. This will be especially true if the opinions of others are solicited confidentially. A list of consultants whose input may be valuable includes professionals already serving the business (i.e., accountant, lawyer, insurance agent, and banker). They do not always need to know the purpose of the due diligence. It can be positioned as an annual review. Their unbiased remarks help sellers see their business for what it really is.

Third, the due diligence will include developing of a business RPM. This can be used to calculate value with the excess earnings and leveraged cash flow methods of business valuation. That is a key benefit. Additionally, an RPM constructed under these low stress conditions is likely to be more well considered, objective and accurate. That is an important resource when a buyer challenges it with one of his or her own.

Assemble Documentation

When a legitimate buyer shows interest, nothing is more impressive than a seller with all the facts at their fingertips. Business owners are equally empowered when prepared to act quickly. There are many documents that can be prepared well in advance of a sale. These include but are not limited to the following:

- ✓ The company business plan (current year)
- ✓ The company marketing plan (if written)
- ✓ Corporate resolutions to list and sell the property
- ✓ Certificates of good standing for a corporation
- ✓ Descriptions of all personal property
- ✓ Fictitious name registration
- ✓ Descriptions of real estate with legal description or a lease

✓ Negotiated options to extend the real estate lease
✓ Good photographs taken on a clear sunny day
✓ A blank note, security agreement and mortgage or deed
✓ A check list of things to do after a buy/sell agreement is accepted
✓ Request forms for credit references and a buyer's personal financial statement
✓ A blank bill of sale
✓ A title report on the real estate (showing it is marketable)
✓ A current franchise operating circular and agreement (if applicable)
✓ Competitive market analysis or intelligence
✓ A list of vendors and key contacts
✓ A customer list
✓ Samples of marketing materials, advertisements, and press clippings, etc.

These and other forms and documents will permit a seller to act as fast as a buyer.

It is a part of the strategy that does not give legitimate buyers a reason to say no. When the time comes, creating documents in advance helps a seller stay focused on running the business while negotiating its sale. Maintaining a calm, confident and organized state of mind at that time is sure to be perceived as a strength.

Business Price

The extra effort to prepare a business for sale pays big dividends in a price that can be substantiated and received. It takes time to do this job right, but the work is small compared to the years of work it takes to build the business. That is of little value without a final effort to maximize the wealth created. Preparation is the key. So, the third aspect for the seller's consideration (in addition to location and condition) is price. This is most important and, fortunately, the one over which sellers have the most control.

When developing a business price in anticipation of a sale, several things are up for discussion. The objective is to weigh the following elements carefully and create an attractive offering.

Best Time to Sell

The bulk of this book is designed to build valuation skill. The question of "how much" is easily answered but "when to sell" is another question of some importance. It has an easy answer too. The best time to sell a business is just before its value reaches a peak. Unfortunately, this is also when most sellers refuse to let go. By this act they could be letting go of a capital gain from a sale whose economic value could be greater than another two or three years of business income.

Prior to a business peak, all systems are go. Trends are positive, as trailing revenue and earnings are steadily increasing. The business enjoys a high profile compared to past activity. Skills that permit business owners to successfully manage the enterprise enable them to predict the near-term future, including how high a peak will be, when it will arrive and how long it will last. If the business is offered after the peak is reached, the trend starts to flatten and isn't as positive. Value declines.

When the trend of business is positive, buyers are more attracted and optimistic. They expect the peak to be farther away that it may actually be. As a result, they are more motivated to act, they will extend themselves a little further and their offers are a little sweeter.

Documenting Results

Anticipate a qualified buyer's request for financial documentation to justify the asking price. Any attempt to finance the purchase price will trigger a request for three to five years of business financial statements and tax returns. What if they don't understand the difference between EBIT and cash flow? Just in case, along with financial statements, build an ERCON (earnings reconstruction) for the past three to five years, too. For each of these years illustrate the difference between EBIT and cash flow. From this it is possible to show trends in trailing revenue, costs and earnings.

It is also a good idea to estimate management compensation since this has an effect on business value (and is used in all valuation methods). The tables in Chapter 4 are a credible and current resource to use. Complement that information with input from local sources. Consider keeping this information private, however, since buyers may be willing to pay a lower level of compensation that a departing seller who's had it all to him or herself.

In addition to the ERCON, build a one-year forecast of revenue, EBIT and cash flow. The company accountant can help. This forecast needs to be as accurate as possible. The success of buyers financed by a seller will depend the quality of the forecast. The goal is to try and identify business "momentum."

Business momentum, using trends and a forecast, is used to build a seller's value range. This is like a buyer's value range but with a small difference. A seller's value range uses business market values created from the current year and a forecast of next year's financial results. Assuming business is increasing, the low value is from this year and the high value is from next year. Sellers should be able to attract buyers with next year's value – asking price – and be prepared to negotiate to this year's value if necessary. This is a conservative approach, but it has the highest odds of producing a good result.

This tactic raises the price, though not so high as to be considered excessive. Buyers will determine for themselves if the asking price is "about to be" justified. Caution: When forecasting earnings, keep these private – marked "not for distribution." When appropriate, give buyers enough information to prepare their own forecasts. Trailing results and basic trend analysis of historical results is sufficient. Otherwise a seller's forecast of future results can be interpreted as a promise of what is to come. There are *no* guarantees.

Target Buyers Pay Most

Two types of buyers for a business exist. The best sales strategy to attract one or the other is to identify which can derive the most benefits from the business offered. Because they have different objectives, this should be taken into consideration when deciding the right benefits to emphasize.

The most frequently encountered small business buyer will be *owner/operators*. They are interested in buying a business and operating it personally. They want employment income and the ability to service acquisition debt until paid under reasonable conditions. A marketing effort to attract this individual should emphasize these benefits. It will also paint a picture of the creative fulfillment available from ownership, since this is a co-benefit of some importance – the sizzle of the steak. Remember, this buyer wants to become free if currently employed. If a practicing entrepreneur is looking for another acquisition, he or she wants to *stay* free. Show them how buying this business satisfies these objectives.

The second, less common buyer is an *investor*. This may also be a practicing entrepreneur, or a larger business on the prowl for good acquisitions. Either seeks growth by nonorganic means – they buy instead of build. To them the creative fulfillment of business ownership is less important; financial results are the priority. Recall the owner/operator wants employment income – management compensation will be an important issue alongside free cash flow to service debt. Investors will be concerned about these points too, but the acquisition is less personal. These buyers normally hire someone else to manage the business. Also, most investors are looking for opportunities that offer *synergy*.

The ability to reduce the costs of management compensation, administration, marketing and production can have a dramatic improvement on EBIT. Moreover, these types of buyers often have more cash and may not need financing. Therefore, free cash flow is measured as a return on investment of cash. As a result, price may be a function of the capitalization rate selected. Investors are more aggressive and select high cap rates. The acceptable asking price can go up when synergy is present. If synergy is added to build cash flow, savings occur improving free cash flow. This can be estimated. The business value can increase because the benefits justify more. For example, suppose synergy creates a savings of $20,000 to a particular investor using an 18% cap rate to value business investments. The indicated value is $221,844. This compares very favorably to the market value of $182,052. Does it include more goodwill? Absolutely. But it is very saleable. Investors recognize the value of intellectual capital. When the numbers fit – they act.

Sellers need to decide early which buyer is most likely to be attracted to their offering. The defining criterion is, surprisingly, not always good financial results. Investors seeking to grow by acquiring more of what they already have may pay a reasonable price. More is paid for acquisitions with synergy and unique, productive intellectual capital. With a few price comparisons, it is possible to target the right buyer.

Make a note: While investors may sometimes pay more, they can be harder to find and tougher to sell. A business must have a high RPM to successfully attract a premium from them. In most cases, the small business opportunity with fewer than 10 employees is best suited to meet the needs of an owner or operator.

Brokers Are a Valuable Resource

Use of brokers to sell a business is an option every business owner should seriously consider. It is true that commissions are saved without them. They may offer benefits, though, that can easily outweigh the direct and indirect costs to sell a business.

Brokers already know the market, and competent ones can quickly evaluate the desirability of a business opportunity. They can make objective recommendations to improve the process and the result. More important, they are already linked up with qualified buyers waiting for a good opportunity. Indeed, they may already know someone ready to act. This can be a real savings of time.

If a buyer is not in place, brokers have already created many marketing mechanisms needed to promote the sale of a business. Recall the favorable estimate of a seller's market in Chapter 13. While true, the best buyers are often not local. This will be particularly the case in rural areas. Local (in this case rural or suburban) investors often remember when the business offered was started or purchased years earlier for much less. This prevents them from making the leap to current day values. Also, local investors are already in the market; moving in is not a motivating factor.

Out-of-area historical precedent does not burden buyers. They are additionally motivated by the desire to relocate. This is especially true of those attempting to move from the city to the country. In an environment where jobs are scarce by comparison, buying a business in a small town is a powerful lure. Properties a local buyer wouldn't take on a bet could be a city buyer's dream come true. Brokers often have the skill and the means to tap into this rich supply. Also, they can do it for less time and cost than a seller not so well positioned. As a result, brokers help sellers get more buyers and negotiate from strength.

Key among the other benefits of brokers is their negotiating skill. They do it for a living. An agent keeps the seller removed from the buyer and the negotiations. They are more objective and their record often shows they attract higher offers. If this were not the case, justification for their fee would not be possible.

Interview potential brokers. Find out how they operate, what resources they bring to the table, their marketing power, their sources of buyers and their valuation experience. Examine their track record of performance and get recommendations. When a broker can be found who offers these resources, retaining their services should be given serious consideration.

Responding to Price Challenges

Preparing a business for sale leads to the point of an offering. The objective is to solicit an offer from a buyer – normally a written one. When it happens preparation is the seller's foundation in dealings with buyers and will start paying dividends.

Qualified and informed buyers build a strong case to support their opinion of business value. They will attempt to get sellers to justify a price. A different set of issues creates anxiety for the novice buyer. He or she can want a lower price without knowing why. In either case, a seller's response sets the tone for continue discussions, if any. It is important to gauge that response, so it is consistent with the situation. Following are a few suggestions for sellers to improve the negotiating environment:

- *Don't overreact.* When an offer is presented, keep an open mind, review the conditions and try to understand the buyer's position. Remember, many buyers are inexperienced entrepreneur wanna-bes. They may be representing themselves at the bargaining table. Like sellers, the way buyers try to protect themselves is with a very low offer. They might be willing to offer more if they could understand why it is justified. It may be necessary to educate them.

- *Don't offer a reaction to a first proposal except to listen.* The first objective is to understand the specific terms and conditions. Learn what there is to work with.

- *Go slow.* Never hesitate to "sleep" on a proposal. This is a reasonable request. A few hours can produce remarkable changes to an initial perspective. First impressions are helpful – but the details can often change a first impression, too. Aggressive expiration dates with an offer are a buyer's attempt to take control of the situation. Ignore them if unreasonable.

- *Convert opinions to offers.* Any buyer interested enough to challenge an asking price is usually an interested buyer. He or she might ask small questions to see how much a seller is willing to negotiate. Shrewd buyers often make verbal offers to test the seller's confidence in price. Here is a word to the wise: "Verbal offers are not worth the paper they aren't written on."

Under most conditions a buyer is not obligated to honor a verbal offer. In the give and take of negotiating, by responding to a verbal offer, the seller indicates a willingness to negotiate and gets little in return. Treat verbal advances as an opportunity to encourage a written offer.

A simple response to a verbal offer testing the business price or terms is to inquire whether buyers are willing to put it in writing. If they are, wait until they do. In other cases buyers may attempt to negotiate peripheral issues verbally, too. To these sellers may encourage *their further discussion when negotiations are captured in writing*. It's an easy way to say, "I'm open, but uncommitted until you are." The act of putting things in writing can strengthen buyers' resolve and commitment to perform.

- *Sell the business*. Remember why buyers want to buy. They want employment income, service debt to create equity – freedom. And the operative word is *"want."* Remind them of how this business can help them accomplish those goals in short order. Remind them of their original objectives. Emphasize favorable business trends. Don't delve too far into specifics or how the price is calculated. Feed the buyer's right brain by sharing some of the creative challenges available and enjoyment of owning a business.

Each small piece of information given to a buyer may mean little if considered separately. Together they build a compelling case to support value and contribute to an overall sense of urgency to buy.

Chapter 15
Trade - Defer Taxes By Exchanging

As previously discussed, a different approach is taken when the same person owns both the business and the real estate. They have more sales options, which can be appealing to potential buyers. Sometimes, and this is especially true in cases of many years of current ownership and in rural areas, the business and real estate are offered as a unit. The capital gain created can be large, so developing a sales strategy that minimizes the effects of taxation is an important consideration.

Note: Information in this chapter includes copyrighted material reprinted with permission from STARKER SERVICES, INC., America's premiere Tax Deferred Exchange third-party intermediary headquartered in Los Gatos, California (800-332-1031). They have 23 service centers located in 18 states to provide nationwide assistance to entrepreneurs and investors seeking to execute tax-deferred exchanges. In addition, as with all other material provided in this text, the material is for informational purposes only and not to be considered legal, accounting or tax advice. The reader is strongly advised to speak with a tax consultant before attempting to employ any of the information or concepts stated herein.

Rather than sell the business or the real estate, it may also be possible to arrange a trade or exchange of properties with another entrepreneur or investor. Exchanges can be made between the business, the business real estate or both, the process is very tax efficient. Internal Revenue Code Section 1031 (IRC 1031) specifically deals with the exchange of investment and business property. The tax code language is straightforward: "No gain or loss shall be recognized on the exchange of property held for productive use in a trade or business or for investment if such property is exchanged solely for property of like-kind which is to be held for productive use in a trade of business or for investment." No gain or loss shall be recognized. With no recognized gain, the taxes are deferred. This type of transaction is called a *tax-deferred exchange*. Any capital gain is deferred until the property exchanged is sold. It creates added equity for the entrepreneur – a major financial benefit.

Business Exchanges

Knowledgeable real estate investors have used IRC Code Sec. 1031 exchanges for many years to avoid capital gains tax on the sale of real property. However, many business proprietors and owners of capital assets have held business property for years because a sale translated into paying many thousands of dollars in capital gains taxes. The advantage of tax deferment available to owners of real estate is also available on the sale of personal property under IRC Code Sec. 1031. Sellers of business assets can exchange into a more desirable or profitable replacement property without losing their equity to capital gains tax.

Tax Rates

The savings potential in exchanging a depreciated property with high residual value, as opposed to selling and paying the taxes, is tremendous. Since business assets are depreciated on a shorter schedule than real estate, depreciation recapture on the sale of personal property is taxed as ordinary income, which could be as high as 39%. In addition, state taxes may be charged.

Restrictions

While the definition of like-kind property for real estate is very broad, the definition for personal property can be very restrictive. Treasury guidelines distinguish between depreciable tangible personal property and other personal property (such as intangible and nondepreciable property). When transferring depreciable business assets, the replacement property must fall into 1) the same "General Asset" class, or 2) the same "Product" class. For example, a truck cannot be exchanged for computer equipment; a plane cannot be exchanged for construction equipment.

ASSET CLASSES

The following is a list of 13 General Asset classes:
- Furniture, fixtures and equipment
- Information systems (computers and peripherals)
- Data handling equipment except computers
- Airplanes (noncommercial fixed wing) and helicopters
- Automobiles and taxis
- Buses
- Light general-purpose trucks
- Heavy general-purpose trucks
- Railroad cars and locomotives (except those owned by railroad transportation companies)
- Over-the-road tractor trailers
- Trailers and trailer-mounted equipment
- Water transportation equipment
- Industrial steam and electric generation and distribution systems

If the property being sold does not fall into the same "General Asset" class as the replacement property, then it should fall into the same "Product " class, published by the Executive Office of Management and Budget, *The Standard*

Industrial Classification Manual defines thousands of very specific asset classifications, sometimes referred to as "SIC Codes." For example, a power crane would have a SIC Code of 3531, and a jet engine 3724.

Intangibles

Intangibles can be considered like-kind to other intangible property. The sale of a business such as a restaurant, hotel or dental practice normally involves intangible personal property, which is generally amortized, straight-line, for 15 years. Examples of intangibles include goodwill, covenants not to compete, franchise licenses, trade names, copyrights, client lists and going concern values.

Tax counsel should be consulted to distinguish the intangibles that can be exchanged from those which cannot. This is an area of considerable controversy, with conflicting case law. Generally, goodwill, covenants not to compete, going concern value and customer lists are not considered property eligible for tax deferral. However, franchises, trademarks, trade names and copyrights, among others, appear to be acceptable exchange property.

Allocation

Exchangers are usually motivated to allocate less value to assets that are non-qualifying – such as goodwill and inventory – to minimize taxable gain. Any allocation must be the same for the seller and the buyer of the property. Consequently, a buyer may not be a willing participant in arbitrary allocation. The IRC has the authority to review unreasonable allocations.

The sale of a business is actually treated as the sale of many assets. The tax code treats a business sale as the sale of each asset falling within a defined group (both tangible and intangible) to determine if there is a gain. All assets of the business must be itemized and placed into the appropriate asset or exchange group. Each exchange group will either have a surplus (if the replacement value is higher) or a deficiency, (if the replacement value is less). There are two ways in which taxable "boot" is typically created: a deficiency (going down in value within a specific exchange group) and a residual group (where any non-matching asset is placed once the total value of the asset groups is determined). Property (including money) within this group also results in taxable boot.

Additional property not eligible for exchange treatment is inventory. The inventory of a business is held for resale and does not fall within the like-kind definition of IRC 1031 property.

Here is an example of a potential business sale/exchange offered by Starker Services, Inc.:

Sample Business Tax Deferred Exchange

A construction company sells for $734,000. Their accountant determines the allocations for the main assets of the company are as follows:

1. Three trucks valued at $33,000 each with an adjusted basis of $15,000
2. One construction crane valued at $170,000 with an adjusted basis of $110,000
3. Two scrapers valued at $70,000 each with an adjusted basis each of $40,000
4. A cement truck valued at $75,000 with an adjusted basis of $50,000
5. A five-year covenant not to compete valued at $25,000 with an adjusted basis of $20,000
6. An airplane (used in normal business) valued at $200,000 with an adjusted basis of $125,000

If the construction company is sold with no exchange, and the fair market value of the equipment is greater than the depreciated basis of the equipment, ownership is facing capital gains taxes. The accountant calculates the gain for each asset class to determine the tax liability. Taxable gain is the variance between value and adjusted basis.

	VALUE	ADJUSTED BASIS	TAXABLE GAIN	TAXABLE GAIN
3 General Purpose Trucks	$ 99,000	$ 45,000	$ 54,000	
1 Crane	$170,000	$110,000	$ 60,000	
2 Scrapers	$140,000	$ 80,000	$ 60,000	
1 Cement Truck	$ 75,000	$ 50,000	$ 25,000	
Goodwill	$ 30,000	$ 15,000		$ 15,000
Covenant not to Compete	$ 25,000	$ 20,000		$ 5,000
Airplane	$200,000	$125,000	$ 75,000	
TOTAL TAXABLE GAINS			$274,000	$ 20,000

An alternative to ownership would be to purchase another construction company in a different location. As a part of the purchase price, they would receive same asset class replacements of equal or greater value, except for the airplane. They must report gain on the sale of intangible assets (excluded property) and the airplane (residual group property). The remaining taxable gain is $199,000. Personal property assets are usually taxed at ordinary income tax rates. Assuming an applicable 31.5% rate the taxes deferred are estimated at $62,685. Ownership may invest this as equity into another like-kind property instead of paying it as capital gains taxes. Employing the concept of the tax-deferred exchange can increase business equity, and ultimately, profitability.

Treasury Regulations

If exchanging an entire business, one asset or the business real estate, general rules will apply. Treasury regulations passed in 1991 allow for the sale of property to give entrepreneurs and real estate investors choosing use IRC 1031 access to benefits described. In general the rules are as follows:

1. Exchangers must identify in writing the property they wish to exchange into (buy) within 45 days from the sale

of their existing property. Identification is made to the intermediary.

2. Exchangers may identify up to three properties they would be interested in purchasing with no limit on value, and they may purchase one, two or all three properties. If they want to identify more than three properties, the gross value of the identified properties cannot be more than 200% of the property being exchanged unless the 95% rule applies.

3. The 95% rule was introduced in Treasury Regulations on April 25, 1991. This regulation states if more than three properties are identified and the aggregate fair market value exceeds 200 of the property being exchanged the exchanger must purchase 95% of the property identified.

4. Exchangers have 180 days from the time they exchange out of their existing property (sold) to the purchase of a new property. Notice this means someone can sell his or her property to one party, allow the sales proceeds to remain in the possession of a qualified third party intermediary, while searching for another. The buyer is not required to have a property that will be exchanged.

5. A qualified intermediary as described in the regulations will be able to handle the other details to ensure the exchange meets IRC-approved format. Individuals having a personal or professional relationship with the exchanger cannot act as their qualified intermediary. With few exceptions, the following are not permitted to act as intermediaries:

   - A family member
   - A controlled corporation, partnership or trust related to the exchanger
   - Anyone considered an agent of the entrepreneur (such as his or her accountant, attorney or real estate agent).

The toughest part of the IRC 1031 exchange as it applies to personal property is the regulation of "like-kind." As generous as the definition is for real (estate) property, it is very narrow when it comes to personal property. This was demonstrated in the construction company example. Use of IRC 1031 to exchange the XYZ Company (without real estate) example would not provide significant benefits to the entrepreneur. This is because goodwill and inventory are likely to be considered the bulk of fair market value exchanged.

Real Estate Exchanges

For real property to be "like-kind" it need only be "property used to produce income, used in a trade or business or held for investment purposes." This broad definition allows entrepreneurs to sell their business separately and exchange the real estate for an apartment building, a rental house, a shopping center or commercial building, an office or industrial building, or for commercial land.

Business owners discovering the high cost of capital gains taxes may want to seriously consider separating business from real estate. Applying the installment sale method to the business and a tax-deferred exchange to the real estate may produce an overall sales strategy that is very tax efficient. Those who own both real estate and business have a unique opportunity to explore this approach.

Taking the simplest approach, the fair market value of XYZ Company's building is $105,000; the adjusted basis is $58,167. Long-term capital gains tax rates are 20%. The deferral of capital gains taxes created by a tax-deferred exchange is calculated as follows. The adjusted basis is subtracted from the building's fair market value to determine the taxable capital gain. This is multiplied by the applicable long-term capital gains tax rate. The result is the amount of taxes that might have been due if not deferred by use of an IRC Code Sec. 1031 Tax-Deferred Exchange. .

Fair Market Value of Real Estate	$105,000
Adjusted Basis	<$ 58,167>
Taxable Capital Gain	$ 46,883
Applicable Tax Rate	20%
Capital Gain Taxes	$ 9,367
Taxes Deferred	$ 9,367

In the original business value placed on the business with real estate, the equity received as a down payment was approximately $30,500. The tax deferred exchange has the potential to increase equity by 31%. This is a sales tactic all sellers with business real estate and qualifying tangible personal property should investigate as a part of their preparation to sell a business.

Chapter 16
Special Situation – Separate the Business From the Real Estate

A special situation occurs when the same entrepreneur owns both a business and the real estate it occupies. In essence, two properties are being sold. Ownership may choose to sell them as a unit or separately. If separately, they must carry different values.

Ownership of both business and real estate is common in small businesses surrounding metropolitan areas and throughout rural America. The strategy separating land from business creates a large reduction in the investment required to own the business. This is especially effective when the expected benefits of ownership are management compensation and payment of acquisition debt.

Sellers also receive important benefits when they separate real estate from business. The most obvious is when the price is lower, more buyers are financially qualified. And creating the largest pool of target buyers helps the business sell faster. In addition, sellers often discover it is just the responsibility of running the business they wish to discard. Ownership of the real estate, however, may remain desirable if reduced to a passive investment. This is particularly true if improvements still have a reasonable amount of book value to depreciate. Simultaneously, ownership could elect to refinance the property and recover equity without selling the real estate at all.

Separating Real Estate from Business Value

Separating business and real estate is easy to do. And calculating the business value afterward is also uncomplicated. The real estate value (easily determined from local market professionals) can be subtracted from the business value and determining the business value (easily determined using the valuation formulas presented earlier in this text), or if preferred, the capitalization formula can be used to determine the investment value of the real estate, which can be deducted from the combined value calculated earlier.

When real estate was included in the business value, no charge was made for rent. Now this must be estimated and included in the business expenses. One method is to examine the rates offered for similar business space and charge a competitive rate. Another is to treat the income required on the investment value of the property as rent. Either way, the rent figure appears as a negative adjustment in the ERCON. In cases where the separation (of business and real estate) occurs, sellers normally offer business buyers a triple-net lease for the real property. This means the lessee pays the cost of all property insurance, taxes, repairs and maintenance. Using this approach it is not necessary to make an additional adjustment to business cash flow for these expenses since they are already included in business expenses.

The adjustment of rent creates an equal reduction of cash flow and free cash flow. The term of financing is shortened to fit the reduced lifespan of personal property securing the debt. The resulting calculations indicate business value without real estate.

To illustrate how the business and real estate values are separated one must know certain variables. Free Cash Flow: $19,932, Market Value of the Real Property: $105,000, Cap Rate: 11.5%.

Next, recall the values developed using the four valuation formulas.

Capitalization Method	$173,322
Excess Earnings Method	$190,782
Leveraged Cash Flow (Seller Financed)	$187,292
Leveraged Cash Flow (Bank Financed)	$177,835

As mentioned, one approach to separation involves subtraction of the market value of the real estate from each price above to produce a new spread of values. This leaves the business with inventory worth $55,000 at cost and approximately $5,000 of fully depreciated furnishings, fixtures and equipment. The new spread of values looks like the following:

Capitalization Method	$ 68,322
Excess Earnings Method	$ 85,782
Leveraged Cash Flow (Seller Financed)	$ 82,292
Leveraged Cash Flow (Bank Financed)	$ 72,825

Recall, Chapter 12 discussed measures of confidence to assess the accuracy of a business value estimate. Using that approach, the business market value indicated is $77,052 with a confidence index of 98.5%. This is very high. However, simply subtracting the value of real estate from business value does not address the issue of affordability. How will cash flow be affected by rent to be paid on the building? And how much should that be? These are important concerns that prompt a more detailed approach.

Reconstructing Business Value Figures

To produce an estimate of business value without real estate, begin by estimating rent. Assume a capitalization rate on the building of 9.75%. This is less than a business cap rate because there is less risk involved. However, it is still 1% over the prime interest rate.

Next, calculate the ROI indicated from a commercial real estate investment worth $105,000 at the selected capitalization rate. The income should be $10,238.

This figure will be treated as rent on the building and applied to the earnings reconstruction as below.

Revenue	$608,951
Cost of Goods	<$397,530>
Gross Profit	$211,421
Expenses	<$190,501>
EBIT (Earnings)	$ 20,920
Depreciation	$ 4,809
Amortization	$ 1,668
EBITDA	$ 27,397
Mortgage Interest	$ 4,533
Non-Recurring Expenses	$ 502
Owner's Salary	$ 18,000
Building Rent	<$ 10,238>
Net Adjustments to EBITDA	$ 12,797
CASH FLOW	$ 40,194

Business cash flow is now $40,194 versus $50,432 when real estate was included. When adjusted for management compensation of $30,500, free cash flow becomes $9,694. Now apply each valuation formula to estimate a new business value.

Capitalization Method

Recall the cap rate for a business is 11.5%. Thus:

$9,694 (I) (11.5% (R) = $84,296 (value w/out real estate)

Excess Earnings Method

Recall the business RPM is 2.57. This stays unchanged, since presumably a buyer would have control over the property by lease. (If anything, the RPM could improve since less investment is made into a less productive asset.) Notice the value calculated using this method is now at the low end of the value range; it was at the high end when real estate is included.

EXCESS EARNINGS METHOD	
Business Free Cash Flow	$ 19,932
Less Rent on Real Estate	<$ 10,238>
Free Cash Flow Without Real Estate	$ 9,694
Tangible Assets	$ 60,000
Safe Rate of Return	6.00%
Return on Tangible Assets	<$ 3,600>
Business Excess Earnings	$ 6,094
Risk/Price Multiple	2.57
Value of Excess Earnings	$ 15,662
Value of Tangible Assets	$ 60,000
ESTIMATED BUSINESS VALUE	$ 65,662

Leveraged Cash Flow Method

The bank financing option is not considered for this exercise because the debt coverage ratio and loan-to-value ratios will reduce financing significantly. For example, an LTV of 50% on inventory and furnishings makes only $30,000 of financing available. Financial leverage is lost unless the seller would carry a second mortgage. Under these conditions, using a loan term and interest rate identical to those offered by a bank, the business estimated value would be the same as if the seller financed the purchase price him or herself. That option is illustrated below. Note, however, even though the business values using seller or bank financed are the same the latter could produce roughly $60,500 of cash at closing if exercised (double the amount produced by the seller-financed option).

LEVERAGED CASH FLOW METHOD
(Seller Financing)

VARIABLES:
Free Cash Flow	$ 19,932	RPM	2.57
Tangible Assets	$165,000	Mgt. Comp.	$30,500

STEP 1: Calculate Monthly Payments For Debt.
Free Cash Flow		$ 9,694.00
(x) Payments per period		12
Monthly Payments		$ 807.83

STEP 2: Determine Amount of Financing.
Interest Rate	9.75%
Loan Term	7
Monthly Payment	$ 807.83
Balance on Due Date	$ 0
Serviceable Debt	$49,041.94

STEP 3: Determine Business Value.
Affordable Loan Balance	$49,071.94
(+) Equity (Mgt. Comp. * 1.00)	$30,500.00
BUSINESS VALUE	$79,041.94

Confidence Index

Recalculating values without real estate will produce the following spread. Since the leveraged cash flows would be the same, only three values are used.

Capitalization Method	$ 84,296
Excess Earnings Method	$ 65,662
Leveraged Cash Flow	$ 79,042

Recalling the formula to measure confidence from Chapter 12, the following variables are calculated:

Mean Value	$ 76,333
Range	$ 18,364
Median of Range	$ 9,317
Market Value of Business	$ 74,979
Variance from Median of Range	$ 1,354
Percent of Variance	1.453
Index of Confidence	85.47%

The index of confidence is now 85%. This compares unfavorably to the 97% calculated when the business included real estate. As a measure designed to build confidence in the value for sellers, the value estimates remain highly reliable. The business will still be as attractive an investment to many owner operators.

Reality Check

The exercise reveals the business market value without real estate is $74,979 (59.9%) less than the business value of $182,052 including real estate. Many more buyers are now capable of making the investment. Notice also an additional seller's benefit is preservation of goodwill. It changed from $17,052 to $14,979, a reduction of only 12%.

The business price without real estate still offers the seller plenty of equity, income from reasonable financing and lease payments on the building. In the future this stream of monthly payments can be used to justify the sale of that asset to another investor. More likely, however, the buyers of the business will seek to acquire it themselves.

Separation of the real estate from the business is a powerful strategy that accomplishes many objectives. It is a special situation all sellers with real estate should strongly consider. It sets the stage to execute an even more attractive method to sell the real estate. That is the subject of a second special situation.

Appendix A
U.S. Department of Labor Household Data Annual Averages

Household Data Annual Averages
Median weekly earnings of full-time wage and salary workers by detailed occupation and sex

Occupation	1999					
	Both Sexes		Men		Women	
	Number of Workers	Median Weekly Earnings	Number of Workers	Median Weekly Earnings	Number of Workers	Median Weekly Earnings
Total, 16 years and over	97,626	$549	55,181	$618	42,444	$473
Managerial and professional specialty	30,704	797	15,537	952	15,167	681
Executive, administrative and managerial	14,973	792	7,981	967	6,992	652
Administrators and officials, public administration	610	877	300	1,007	310	725
Administrators, protective services	55	889	44	(1)	11	(1)
Financial managers	697	878	344	1,154	353	703
Personnel and labor relations managers	181	831	74	1,014	108	742
Purchasing managers	139	803	74	989	65	699
Managers, marketing, advertising and public relations	695	1,036	441	1,241	254	800
Administrators, education and related fields	703	913	282	1,076	420	819
Managers, medicine and health	602	759	139	1,006	462	714
Managers, food servings and lodging establishments	946	524	498	617	449	461
Managers, properties and real estate	338	600	149	679	189	578
Management-related occupations	4,026	704	1,677	847	2,349	630
Accountants and auditors	1,362	723	549	891	813	651
Underwriters	119	744	39	(1)	80	653
Other financial officers	684	758	324	923	360	615
Management analysts	244	908	126	1,080	118	790
Personnel, training and labor relations specialists	475	674	149	727	326	653
Buyers, wholesale and retail trade, except farm products	140	643	75	675	65	588
Construction inspectors	67	730	63	748	4	(1)
Inspectors and compliance officers, except construction	234	755	161	772	73	707

Household Data Annual Averages

Median weekly earnings of full-time wage and salary workers by detailed occupation and sex

Occupation	Both Sexes		Men		Women	
	Number of Workers	Median Weekly Earnings	Number of Workers	Median Weekly Earnings	Number of Workers	Median Weekly Earnings
Professional speciality	15,731	$800	7,556	$939	8,175	707
Engineers, architects and surveyors	2,084	1,033	1,865	1,052	219	907
Architects	129	918	108	983	21	(1)
Engineers	1,945	1,041	1,749	1,058	197	933
Aerospace engineers	84	1,201	74	1202	10	(1)
Chemical engineers	75	1,260	62	1,312	13	(1)
Civil engineers	255	965	229	984	25	(1)
Electrical and electronic engineers	618	1,073	564	1,087	55	956
Industrial engineers	259	970	216	991	43	(1)
Mechanical engineers	324	1,035	304	1,041	19	(1)
Mathematical and computer scientists	1,638	983	1,117	1,056	522	876
Computer systems analysts and scientists	1,348	1,008	959	1,079	390	907
Operations and systems researchers and analysts	242	864	128	952	115	781
Natural scientists	514	873	370	939	143	731
Chemists, except biochemists	131	970	100	1,002	31	(1)
Physical scientists, n.e.c.	50	987	38	(1)	12	(1)
Biological and life scientists	95	762	52	801	42	(1)
Medical scientists	93	724	54	800	38	(1)
Health diagnosing occupations	539	1,192	389	1,342	150	888
Physicians	460	1,266	335	1,364	125	852
Health assessment and treating occupations	2,219	760	368	887	1,851	746
Registered nurses	1,585	750	141	791	1,443	747

Household Data Annual Averages
Median weekly earnings of full-time wage and salary workers by detailed occupation and sex

Occupation	Both Sexes		1999 Men		Women	
	Number of Workers	Median Weekly Earnings	Number of Workers	Median Weekly Earnings	Number of Workers	Median Weekly Earnings
Pharmacists	165	$1,159	88	1,222	77	$1,105
Dietitians	55	577	8	(1)	47	(1)
Therapists	356	728	101	793	256	707
Respiratory therapists	69	689	31	(1)	38	(1)
Physical therapists	86	877	28	(1)	58	808
Speech therapists	65	780	5	(1)	61	770
Physicians' assistants	58	908	29	(1)	29	(1)
Teachers, college and university	638	953	397	1,038	241	859
Teachers, except college and university	4,259	688	1,130	768	3,129	659
Teachers, prekindergarten and kindergarten	432	440	9	(1)	423	442
Teachers, elementary school	1,837	710	308	785	1,529	697
Teachers, secondary school	1,179	756	521	803	658	722
Teachers, special education	326	677	53	744	273	664
Counselors, educational and vocational	207	786	62	902	144	742
Librarians, archivists, and curators	210	701	39	(1)	171	684
Librarians	183	700	32	(1)	151	684
Social scientists and urban planners	306	740	142	847	164	682
Economists	120	863	57	977	63	774
Psychologists	141	673	55	760	86	623
Social, recreation and religious workers	1,177	596	542	654	634	557
Social workers	705	601	220	661	485	579
Recreation workers	85	416	27	(1)	58	417

Household Data Annual Averages

Median weekly earnings of full-time wage and salary workers by detailed occupation and sex

Occupation	Both Sexes		Men		Women	
	Number of Workers	Median Weekly Earnings	Number of Workers	Median Weekly Earnings	Number of Workers	Median Weekly Earnings
Clergy	295	$657	256	676	38	(1)
Lawyers and judges	613	1,198	412	1,369	201	971
Lawyers	577	1,168	386	1,340	191	974
Writers, artists, entertainers and athletes	1,327	681	722	748	604	605
Technical writers	63	861	25	(1)	38	(1)
Designers	453	642	233	757	220	512
Actors and directors	65	784	45	(1)	20	(1)
Painters, sculptors, craft artists and artist printmakers	93	595	52	647	41	(1)
Photographers	56	617	47	(1)	9	(1)
Editors and reporters	212	750	113	803	98	709
Public relations specialists	155	735	58	881	97	684
Athletes	54	613	46	(1)	8	(1)
Technical, sales and administrative support	27,388	488	10,525	626	16,863	431
Technicians and related support	3,550	618	1,802	728	1,749	528
Health technologists and technicians	1,304	511	292	594	1,011	489
Clinical laboratory technologists and technicians	292	623	77	709	215	593
Radiologic technicians	139	619	40	(1)	99	596
Licensed practical nurses	259	498	16	(1)	243	492
Engineering and related technologists and technicians	874	662	716	673	158	625
Electrical and electronic technicians	412	690	348	701	64	649
Drafting occupations	212	665	177	663	35	(1)

Household Data Annual Averages
Median weekly earnings of full-time wage and salary workers by detailed occupation and sex

Occupation	1999							
	Both Sexes			Men			Women	
	Number of Workers	Median Weekly Earnings		Number of Workers	Median Weekly Earnings		Number of Workers	Median Weekly Earnings
Surveying and mapping technicians	51	$557		44	(1)		7	(1)
Science Technicians	250	582		150	656		100	480
Biological technicians	86	500		36	(1)		50	388
Chemical technicians	71	677		46	(1)		25	(1)
Technicians, except health, engineering and science	1,122	761		643	902		479	624
Airplane pilots and navigators	99	1,048		97	1,050		3	(1)
Computer programmers	564	898		405	935		159	788
Legal Assistants	313	589		43	(1)		270	581
Sales occupations	9,728	523		5,402	666		4,326	399
Supervisors and proprietors	3,275	587		1,924	691		1,351	454
Sales representatives, finance and business services	1,817	708		1,019	821		798	589
Insurance sales	391	622		201	750		190	539
Real estate sales	364	657		173	767		191	585
Securities and financial services sales	399	791		276	979		123	616
Advertising and related sales	155	747		66	892		88	626
Sales occupations, other business services	508	721		302	809		206	611
Sales representatives, commodities, except retail	1,279	749		968	792		311	610
Sales workers, retail and personal services	3,324	329		1,475	423		1,849	296
Sales workers, motor vehicles and boats	268	665		240	679		29	(1)
Sales workers, apparel	148	298		43	(1)		104	286
Sales workers, shoes	57	302		33	(1)		24	(1)

Household Data Annual Averages

Median weekly earnings of full-time wage and salary workers by detailed occupation and sex

	1999								
	Both Sexes			Men			Women		
Occupation	Number of Workers	Median Weekly Earnings		Number of Workers	Median Weekly Earnings		Number of Workers	Median Weekly Earnings	
Sales workers, furniture and home furnishings	118	$511		62	536		57	497	
Sales workers, radio, television, hi-fi and appliances	213	495		157	512		56	413	
Sales workers, hardware and building supplies	204	426		163	473		41	(1)	
Sales workers, parts	146	400		132	403		15	(1)	
Sales workers, other commodities	645	333		249	392		396	315	
Sales counter clerks	94	335		34	(1)		60	303	
Cashiers	1,289	280		301	296		989	275	
Street and door-to-door sales workers	117	431		47	(1)		70	387	
Administrative support, including clerical	14,109	447		3,322	539		10,788	427	
Supervisors	650	603		282	701		368	560	
General office	348	595		115	706		233	539	
Financial records processing	77	678		15	(1)		62	622	
Distribution, scheduling and adjusting clerks	207	590		140	668		67	511	
Computer equipment operators	298	525		128	610		170	485	
Computer operators	292	528		124	612		168	485	
Secretaries, stenographers and typists	2,629	446		47	(1)		2,582	446	
Secretaries	2,162	443		26	(1)		2,136	443	
Stenographers	67	490		4	(1)		63	488	
Typists	400	454		17	(1)		382	455	
Information Clerks	1,467	393		182	497		1,285	386	
Inteviewers	120	408		17	(1)		103	396	

Household Data Annual Averages

Median weekly earnings of full-time wage and salary workers by detailed occupation and sex

Occupation	Both Sexes		Men		Women	
	Number of Workers	Median Weekly Earnings	Number of Workers	Median Weekly Earnings	Number of Workers	Median Weekly Earnings
Hotel clerks	89	$315	22	(1)	67	$308
Transportation ticket and reservation agents	218	486	70	527	147	464
Receptionists	727	374	30	(1)	697	373
Records processing, except financial	753	440	171	513	582	421
Order clerks	249	493	70	629	179	460
Personnel clerks, except payroll and timekeeping	58	523	10	(1)	49	(1)
Library clerks	58	434	15	(1)	43	(1)
File clerks	206	361	43	(1)	162	349
Record clerks	174	437	32	(1)	142	423
Financial records processing	1,480	440	157	489	1,322	435
Bookkeeprs, accounting and auditing clerks	1,084	443	107	478	977	440
Payroll and timekeeping clerks	127	474	16	(1)	111	459
Billing clerks	145	428	14	(1)	131	428
Billing, posting and calculating machine operators	74	404	10	(1)	63	400
Communications equipment operators	117	384	29	(1)	88	367
Telephone operators	107	377	24	(1)	83	365
Mail and message distributing	829	629	504	665	325	575
Postal clerks, except mail carriers	298	687	156	701	142	670
Mail carriers, postal service	301	697	218	714	82	646
Mail clerks, except postal service	135	389	50	414	85	382
Messengers	96	453	80	457	16	(1)
Material recording, scheduling and distributing clerks	1,652	448	953	485	700	417
Dispatchers	232	487	107	583	125	441

Household Data Annual Averages

Median weekly earnings of full-time wage and salary workers by detailed occupation and sex

Occupation	Both Sexes		Men		Women	
	Number of Workers	Median Weekly Earnings	Number of Workers	Median Weekly Earnings	Number of Workers	Median Weekly Earnings
Production coordinators	181	$592	71	734	109	$474
Traffic, shipping and receiving clerks	572	411	409	419	163	388
Stock and inventory clerks	398	470	242	505	156	438
Expediters	191	393	65	487	126	364
Adjusters and investigators	1,596	473	400	536	1,196	453
Insurance adjusters, examiners and investigators	416	528	112	660	304	501
Investigators and adjusters, except insurance	925	452	219	511	706	435
Eligibility clerks, social welfare	98	481	13	(1)	85	468
Bill and account collectors	157	451	56	489	101	429
Miscellaneous administrative support occupations	2,593	409	448	483	2,145	399
General office clerks	511	419	98	461	412	413
Bank tellers	288	346	21	(1)	267	343
Data-entry keyers	594	422	110	433	484	420
Statistical clerks	80	432	17	(1)	63	401
Teachers' aides	368	315	28	(1)	341	314
Service occupations	10,841	336	5,209	402	5,632	304
Private household	384	243	17	(1)	367	240
Child care workers	157	211	1	(1)	156	212
Cleaners and servants	220	259	15	(1)	205	255
Protective services	2,138	592	1,791	613	347	492
Supervisors	180	759	156	815	23	(1)

Household Data Annual Averages
Median weekly earnings of full-time wage and salary workers by detailed occupation and sex

Occupation	Both Sexes		1999 Men		Women	
	Number of Workers	Median Weekly Earnings	Number of Workers	Median Weekly Earnings	Number of Workers	Median Weekly Earnings
Police and detectives	100	$817	84	$889	16	(1)
Firefighting and fire prevention	221	740	216	742	5	(1)
Firefighting	204	744	202	745	3	(1)
Police and detectives	1,079	657	898	681	181	574
Police and detectives, public service	602	751	519	766	83	650
Sheriffs, bailiffs and other law enforcement officers	179	628	153	645	27	(1)
Correction institution officers	298	521	226	540	72	492
Guards	659	393	521	402	138	335
Guards and police, except public service	618	398	501	403	118	368
Service occupations, except private household and protective	8,318	313	3,400	336	4,918	302
Food preparation and service occupations	3,189	298	1,583	311	1,607	286
Supervisors	276	342	120	415	156	310
Bartenders	167	334	97	334	70	334
Waiters and waitresses	652	302	172	325	480	294
Cooks, except short order	1,311	302	800	317	511	279
Food counter, fountain and related occupations	108	252	46	(1)	62	247
Kitchen workers, food preparation	135	297	41	(1)	94	295
Waiters' and waitresses' assistants	229	286	119	290	110	282
Miscellaneous food preparation occupations	312	268	188	266	124	270
Health service occupations	1,791	324	217	368	1,574	320
Dental assistants	127	377	5	(1)	123	373

Household Data Annual Averages

Median weekly earnings of full-time wage and salary workers by detailed occupation and sex

Occupation	1999								
	Both Sexes		Men		Women	
	Number of Workers	Median Weekly Earnings	Number of Workers	Median Weekly Earnings	Number of Workers	Median Weekly Earnings
Health aides, except nursing	246	$318	49	(1)	196	$317
Nursing aides, orderlies and attendants	1,418	322	163	367	1,255	318
Cleaning and building service occupations	2,188	321	1,303	363	885	292
Supervisors	153	407	97	472	55	317
Maids and housemen	472	296	87	330	385	289
Janitors and cleaners	1,496	324	1,054	351	442	293
Pest control	59	450	56	450	2	(1)
Personal service occupations	1,150	321	298	379	852	310
Supervisors	56	470	24	(1)	32	(1)
Hairdressers and cosmetologists	310	322	47	(1)	263	323
Attendants, amusement and recreation facilities	140	384	83	384	57	384
Public transportation attendants	58	604	11	(1)	47	(1)
Welfare service aides	54	310	6	(1)	49	(1)
Early childhood teachers' assistants	266	275	10	(1)	256	274
Precision production, craft and repair	11,927	594	10,861	606	1,066	428
Mechanics and repairers	4,263	621	4,057	622	206	592
Supervisors	262	816	232	820	30	(1)
Mechanics and repairers, except supervisors	4,001	613	3,824	615	176	555
Vehicles and mobile equipment mechanics and repairers	1,455	594	1,436	594	18	(1)
Automobile mechanics	635	555	628	555	7	(1)
Bus, truck and stationary engine mechanics	301	588	300	588	1	(1)

Household Data Annual Averages

Median weekly earnings of full-time wage and salary workers by detailed occupation and sex

Occupation	1999					
	Both Sexes		Men		Women	
	Number of Workers	Median Weekly Earnings	Number of Workers	Median Weekly Earnings	Number of Workers	Median Weekly Earnings
Aircraft engine mechanics	146	$737	142	$740	4	(1)
Small engine repairers	54	420	53	419	2	(1)
Automobile body and related repairers	123	584	121	586	1	(1)
Heavy equipment mechanics	145	667	144	669	1	(1)
Industrial machinery repairers	546	608	530	612	16	(1)
Electrical and electronic equipment repairers	889	698	785	703	104	616
Electronic repairers, communications and industrial	201	621	184	630	17	(1)
Data processing equipment repairers	281	689	233	707	48	(1)
Telephone line installers and repairers	55	755	51	760	3	(1)
Telephone installers and repairers	240	770	210	761	30	(1)
Miscellaneous electrical/electronic equipment repairers	74	693	70	694	4	(1)
Heating, air conditioning and refrigeration mechanics	310	580	308	579	2	(1)
Miscellaneous mechanics and repairers	790	607	754	612	36	(1)
Millwrights	72	697	70	700	2	(1)
Construction trades	4,143	566	4,059	571	85	423
Supervisors	504	720	495	722	9	(1)
Construction trades, except supervisors	3,639	540	3,563	545	76	417
Brickmasons and stonemasons	128	546	125	564	3	(1)
Tile setters, hard and soft	58	440	56	443	2	(1)
Carpet installers	62	507	62	507		
Carpenters	962	518	950	518	12	(1)
Drywall installers	126	483	121	486	5	(1)

Household Data Annual Averages

Median weekly earnings of full-time wage and salary workers by detailed occupation and sex

Occupation	Both Sexes		1999 Men		Women	
	Number of Workers	Median Weekly Earnings	Number of Workers	Median Weekly Earnings	Number of Workers	Median Weekly Earnings
Electricians	739	$645	723	651	17	(1)
Electrical power installers and repairers	134	731	133	730	1	(1)
Painters, construction and maintenance	331	427	317	432	14	(1)
Plumbers, pipefitters, steamfitters and apprentices	417	595	408	596	9	(1)
Concrete and terrazzo finishers	87	501	85	501	2	(1)
Insulation workers	51	546	49	(1)	2	(1)
Roofers	147	467	146	469	1	(1)
Structural metal workers	55	634	55	634		
Extractive occupations	128	716	126	717	2	(1)
Precision production occupations	3,393	583	2,619	630	774	403
Supervisors	1,121	668	904	704	217	515
Precision metalworking occupations	869	634	809	646	60	442
Tool and die makers	139	785	134	792	5	(1)
Machinists	489	604	461	610	28	(1)
Sheet-metal workers	128	628	120	635	8	(1)
Precision woodworking occupations	75	457	65	481	11	(1)
Cabinet makers and bench carpenters	58	454	54	465	4	(1)
Precision textile, apparel and furnishings machine workers	115	402	65	421	50	350
Precision workers, assorted materials	460	423	203	513	257	369
Optical goods workers	64	465	26	(1)	38	(1)
Electrical and electronic equipment assemblers	290	391	97	476	193	359
Precision food production occupations	380	400	242	440	138	342

Household Data Annual Averages

Median weekly earnings of full-time wage and salary workers by detailed occupation and sex

	1999							
	Both Sexes			Men			Women	
Occupation	Number of Workers	Median Weekly Earnings		Number of Workers	Median Weekly Earnings		Number of Workers	Median Weekly Earnings
Butchers and meat cutters	237	$400		174	$428		64	$322
Bakers	110	394		61	475		49	(1)
Precision inspectors, testers and related workers	131	618		100	657		32	(1)
Inspectors, testers and graders	123	619		94	654		30	(1)
Plant and system operators	241	688		233	689		9	(1)
Water and sewage treatment plant operators	56	625		53	635		4	(1)
Stationary engineers	109	621		109	620			
Operators, fabricators and laborers	15,182	429		11,685	472		3,498	337
Machine operators, assemblers and inspectors	6,814	423		4,371	487		2,444	340
Machine operators and tenders, except precision	4,368	416		2,829	481		1,538	326
Metalworking and plastic working machine operators	369	509		307	534		62	410
Punching and stamping press machine operators	101	458		74	505		27	(1)
Grinding, abrading, buffing and polishing operators	113	490		97	507		16	(1)
Metal and plastic processing machine operators	142	454		110	471		32	(1)
Molding and casting machine operators	97	452		74	473		23	(1)
Woodworking machine operators	138	385		119	398		19	(1)
Sawing machine operators	81	386		71	393		10	(1)
Printing machine operators	325	491		251	526		74	366
Printing press operators	256	477		208	513		48	(1)
Textile, apparel and furnishings machine operators	745	298		211	348		534	282
Textile sewing machine operators	416	282		94	326		322	273

Household Data Annual Averages
Median weekly earnings of full-time wage and salary workers by detailed occupation and sex

Occupation	Both Sexes		Men		Women	
	Number of Workers	Median Weekly Earnings	Number of Workers	Median Weekly Earnings	Number of Workers	Median Weekly Earnings
			1999			
Pressing machine operators	67	$268	17	(1)	50	$260
Laundering and dry cleaning machine operators	139	294	48	(1)	90	266
Machine operators, assorted materials	2,622	437	1,813	487	809	350
Packaging and filling machine operators	341	361	129	416	212	327
Mixing and blending machine operators	129	491	112	497	16	(1)
Separating, filtering and clarifying machine operators	58	648	50	657	8	(1)
Painting and paint spraying machine operators	186	462	161	480	25	(1)
Furnace, kiln and over operators, excluding food	69	591	67	597	2	(1)
Slicing and cutting machine operators	153	430	115	473	38	(1)
Photographic process machine operators	69	342	34	(1)	35	(1)
Fabricators, assemblers and hand working occupations	1,781	444	1,192	495	589	365
Welders and cutters	527	520	496	525	32	(1)
Assemblers	1,158	412	637	463	521	368
Production inspectors, testers, samplers and weighers	665	424	349	506	316	369
Production inspectors, checkers and examiners	487	456	256	530	231	395
Production testers	53	520	39	(1)	14	(1)
Graders and sorters, except agricultural	120	305	52	347	69	288
Transportation and material moving occupations	4,401	513	4,083	522	317	394
Motor vehicle operators	3,184	514	2,927	524	257	389
Supervisors	78	585	61	621	17	(1)
Truck Drivers	2,493	527	2,409	532	85	412

Household Data Annual Averages
Median weekly earnings of full-time wage and salary workers by detailed occupation and sex

Occupation	Both Sexes		Men		Women	
	Number of Workers	Median Weekly Earnings	Number of Workers	Median Weekly Earnings	Number of Workers	Median Weekly Earnings
Drivers - sales workers	130	$534	122	$555	8	(1)
Bus drivers	284	428	166	498	119	384
Taxicab drivers and chauffeurs	149	427	127	441	22	(1)
Transportation occupations, except motor vehicles	154	761	152	772	2	(1)
Rail transportation	108	816	107	820	1	(1)
Material moving equipment operators	1,063	498	1,005	503	58	415
Operating engineers	229	575	223	579	6	(1)
Crane and tower operators	69	580	67	586	2	(1)
Excavating and loading machine operators	81	571	79	577	2	(1)
Grader, dozer and scraper operators	63	480	61	477	2	(1)
Industrial truck and tractor equipment operators	513	448	474	451	39	(1)
Handlers, equipment cleaners, helpers and laborers	3,967	363	3,230	377	737	314
Helpers, construction and extractive occupations	106	329	103	330	3	(1)
Helpers, construction trades	93	336	92	335	2	(1)
Construction laborers	804	414	776	413	28	(1)
Production helpers	53	357	42	(1)	11	(1)
Freight, stock and material handlers	1,287	361	996	375	291	318
Stock handlers and baggers	578	314	389	320	189	300
Machine feeders and offbearers	75	395	45	(1)	30	(1)
Garage and service station related occupations	134	314	131	313	3	(1)
Vehicle washers and equipment cleaners	199	312	173	315	26	(1)

Household Data Annual Averages

Median weekly earnings of full-time wage and salary workers by detailed occupation and sex

Occupation	Both Sexes		Men		Women	
	Number of Workers	Median Weekly Earnings	Number of Workers	Median Weekly Earnings	Number of Workers	Median Weekly Earnings
			1999			
Hand packers and packagers	253	$317	107	$338	147	305
Laborers, except construction	1,107	373	879	393	229	315
Farming, forestry and fishing	1,583	331	1,364	341	218	283
Farm operators and managers	72	499	61	525	11	(1)
Farm managers	67	499	56	543	11	(1)
Other agricultural and related occupations	1,441	321	1,237	329	204	277
Farm occupations, except managerial	603	311	512	317	91	268
Farm workers	531	304	463	311	68	259
Related agricultural occupations	838	330	725	342	113	288
Supervisors, related agricultural	87	514	81	539	6	(1)
Groundskeepers and gardeners, except farm	657	322	614	322	44	(1)
Forestry and logging occupations	58	503	55	508	2	(1)

(1) Data not shown where base is less than 50,000.

NOTE: Beginning in January 1999, data reflect revised population controls used in the household survey.

Household Data Annual Averages | **203**

Appendix B
Business Valuation Formulas & Forms

Shortcut To Estimate Cash Flow

This technique is used to develop a rough estimate of a business cash flow with limited information. It works well because sellers do not feel answers to questions asked will be too revealing. Knowing how to calculate cost of goods from revenue and a percent markup is the key. This technique is fully described in Chapter Three. To develop the estimate the entrepreneur asks three questions and performs four simple steps listed below. Answers may be received by asking a seller during an initial meeting.

- "How much is the average revenue per month?"
- "What is the average markup on merchandise sold?"
- "On average, what are the cash expenses of the business, excluding owner's salary, each month?"

STEP 1: Calculate Cost of Goods.

Revenue ÷ 1.00 + Percent of Markup = Cost of Goods

$50,000 ÷ 1.00 + .30 (130%) = $38,451.64

STEP 2: Calculate Business Gross Profit.

Revenue – Cost of Goods = Gross Profit

$50,000 - $38,451.63 = $11,538.46

STEP 3: Calculate Estimate of Business Cash Flow.

Gross Profit – Expenses = Cash Flow

$11,538.46 - $6,000 = $5,538.46

STEP 4: Estimate Annual Cash Flow.

Monthly Cash Flow x Months Per Year = Annual Cash Flow

$5,538.46 x 12 = $66,461.53

ERCON

Revenue		$_____
Cost of Goods	<$_____>	
Gross Profit		$_____
Expenses	<$_____>	
EBIT (Earnings Before Income Taxes)		$_____
Depreciation		$_____
Amortization		$_____
EBITDA		$_____
Positive Adjustments		
Education		$_____
Employee Benefits		$_____
Entertainment		$_____
Home Office		$_____
Mortgage Interest		$_____
Non-Recurring Expenses		$_____
Payroll (Owners Plus/Minus Other)		$_____
Transportation		$_____
Travel		$_____
_____		$_____
_____		$_____
_____		$_____
Negative Adjustments		
_____	<$_____>	
_____	<$_____>	
_____	<$_____>	
Net Adjustments		$_____
<u>BUSINESS CASH FLOW</u>		$_____

Business RPM Calculator

FINANCE _____
    Trailing Revenue
    Revenue Momentum
    Capital Structure _____
    Leverage Opportunities _____
    Earnings & Cash Flow _____

CONTROL _____
    Employee Turnover Rate & Cost (ETOR/ETOC)
    Employee Compensation _____
    Contingency Planning _____
    Network Penetration _____
    Potential Litigation _____

MARKETING _____
    Well-Defined Marketing Plan _____
    Branded Power _____
    Market Differentiation _____
    Market Segmentation _____
    E-Commerce Activity _____

SALES _____
    Type of Service or Product
    Sales Process Fit _____
    Sales Incentives Available _____
    Sales Training Programs _____
    Wired Distribution _____

PRODUCTION _____
    Emphasis on Quality _____
    Innovation _____
    Capacity vs Demand _____
    Obsolescence _____
    Inventory Management _____

SERVICE _____
    Integrated Vision _____
    Employee Recognition _____
    Team Spirit _____
    Flexibility _____
    Open Communication _____

INTELLECTUAL CAPITAL _____
    Customer Satisfaction _____
    Employee Motivation _____
    Potential Synergies _____
    Key People _____
    Institutional Intelligence _____

BUSINESS RPM _____

CAPITALIZATION METHOD

I (income) $_____ R (rate) _____%
V (value) $_____

$$\frac{I}{R \times V}$$

Note#1

- Income divided by Rate equals Value (I ÷ R=V)
- Income divided by Value equals Rate (I ÷ V=R)
- Rate times Value equals Income (R x V=I)

Note #2

To calculate business values when one is not given, select a capitalization rate. Use free cash flow as Income.

To challenge a given business value solve for rate. Compare this to investor expectations. Or, solve for income and compare it to the actual free cash flow available.

When differences between expected and actual rate/income exist substitute the market rate expected for the rate offered and solve for the indicated business value.

Excess Earnings Method

VARIABLES
Free Cash Flow $_____   Safe Rate _____%
Tangible Assets $_____   RPM   _____

Business Free Cash Flow $_____

Tangible Assets $_____
(x) <u>Safe Rate of Return</u>   _____%
Return on Tangible Assets $_____ <$_____>

Business Excess Earnings $_____
(x) <u>Risk/Price Multiple</u>   _____
Value of Excess Earnings $_____
(+) Value of Tangible Assets $_____

<u>ESTIMATED BUSINESS VALUE</u> $_____

Excess Earnings Challenge

Business Value $_____
(-) <u>Market Value of Tangible Assets</u>   <$_____>
Value of Excess Earnings $_____

<u>Value of Excess Earnings</u> $_____
(÷) <u>Amount of Excess Earnings</u> $_____
Risk/Price Multiple   _____

Note #1
Substitute Actual RPM for indicated and recalculate
value of excess earnings and business value.

Leveraged Cash Flow Method

VARIABLES

Free Cash Flow $_____   RPM   _____

Tangible Assets $_____   Mgt. Comp. $_____

STEP 1: Calculate Monthly Payments For Debt.

Free Cash Flow	$_____
(÷) <u>Payments Per Period</u>	_____
Monthly Payments	$_____

STEP 2: Determine Amount of Financing.

Interest Rate	_____%
Loan Term	_____
Monthly Payment	$_____
Balance on Due Date	$_____
Serviceable Debt	$_____

STEP 3: Determine Business Value.

Affordable Loan Balance	$_____
(+) <u>Equity (Mgt. Comp. * (___)</u>	$_____
BUSINESS VALUE	$_____

Note #1

Substitute variables and terms of finance and recalculate for value. Compare against the asking price to challenge its accuracy.

Confidence Index Calculation

BUSINESS VALUES:

    Capitalization $\$$_____   LCF–Seller Financed $\$$_____

    Excess Earnings $\$$_____   LCF-Bank Financed $\$$_____

STEP 1: Calculate the Mean of Values.

Total of Values	$\$$_____
(÷) No. of Values	_____
Mean (M)	$\$$_____

STEP 2: Calculate the Range.

BV^H	$\$$_____
(-) BV^L	$\$$_____
Range	$\$$_____

STEP 3: Calculate the Median of the Range.

Range	$\$$_____
(÷) One-Half the Range	_____
Median (MD)	$\$$_____

STEP 4: Calculate Market Value.

Median (MD)	$\$$_____
(+) BV^L	$\$$_____
Market Value	$\$$_____

STEP 5: Calculate Variance (M and MV).

Mean (M)	$\$$_____
(-) Market Value	<$\$$_____>
Variance	$\$$_____

STEP 6: Convert Variance to a Percent of the Range.

Variance	$\$$_____
(÷) Median (MD)	$\$$_____
Percent of Variance	_____

STEP 7: Calculate Confidence Index.

Percents Available	1.00
(-) Percent of Variance	_____

<u>CONFIDENCE INDEX</u>   _____

Appendix C
Checklist Of Tax Terms and Issues

The United States Tax Code has many regulations that can change and, sometimes, frequently and with little notice. Building tax efficient strategies has the potential to minimize taxes and maximize profits. Entrepreneurs should develop a general awareness of tax strategies that work to their advantage and minimize the impact of taxes. This material and information is not given as tax advice nor is it to be used as such. As with all information presented in this text readers are advised to seek the guidance of qualified professional representative or accountant.

The following is a checklist of some tax issues that may affect business acquisition, ownership and disposition. It includes a brief description of each item. Note, the tax code is several million pages. This material is for general information purposes only. It is intended to acquaint the reader with general concepts that may apply to business acquisition, management and dispositions. Prior to application a qualified tax accountant or attorney should be consulted.

Taxable Income

• **Tax Rates.** Tax rates are the percent of qualifying income received in the fiscal or calendar year that will be paid in taxes.

Tax rates vary according to the type of taxpayer. There are different rates for corporations, individual taxpayers, heads of households, and married taxpayers filing together or separately.

The current range of corporate tax rates is graduated from 15 percent to 39 percent. Corporate tax rates for most individuals the range of tax rates is graduated from 15 percent to 39.6 percent. EBIT, or taxable earnings, produced by most small businesses is often passed to ownership based on their prorated interest in the company. When business income is credited to owners it is taxed according to their individual applicable tax rate.

• **Taxable Income – Cash Basis.** A business owner's method of accounting will determine the year in which income is considered taxable. The cash basis of accounting is used by most small businesses. With this method income is earned and taxable in same year it is received.

• **Taxable Income – Accrual Method.** Income that becomes taxable when earned is an example of the accrual method of accounting. Income is earned when services or goods necessary to be exchanged for income have been delivered. Notice, with this method it is possible to earn income taxable without receiving the actual income until a later taxable year.

• **Capital Gains & Losses.** A capital gain or loss occurs upon the sale of a capital asset. IRC 1221 states what are not capital assets. This list includes business property such as inventory, depreciable business property, and business land not held for investment. The code attempts to distinguish between gains arising from capital appreciation versus normal business activity. The sale of inventory is considered business profit not capital gain. The gain on antiques held for their investment potential may be a capital gain.

Capital gains are divided into two categories: short-term capital gain; and long-term capital gain. The difference is created by the holding period. Generally, long-term capital gains receive more favorable tax treatment. The long-term capital gains tax rate for individual taxpayers is 20%. This compares very favorably to the higher rates that apply to ordinary income. A short-term capital gain is taxed the same as ordinary income.

• **Net Operating Losses.** Net operating losses in a business occur when business expenses exceed the income for a taxable year. IRC 172. Net operating losses can be carried back to offset income received in previous years creating a refund for the taxpayer. Or, net operating losses can be carried forward and deducted from the income created in a future year. The result is a savings of taxes.

• **Passive Losses.** Passive losses may occur with investments in which the entrepreneur does not play a material role or actively participate. Examples of passive income investments are apartment buildings and other types of commercial real estate investments. Prior to 1987 it was possible for high-income taxpayers to use a net operating loss from passive investments to offset income earned from their business or profession. The result was a savings of taxes. Passive investments providing net operating losses were called tax shelters.

IRC 469 states that the use of losses or tax credits created by passive investment activity cannot be used to reduce tax liability created by business income earned.

Taxable Treatment Of Transactions

• **Sale or Exchange of Property.** A sale of a property occurs when one receives cash, notes, or their equivalent in exchange for ownership of a property (IRC 1222). An exchange occurs when one receives other property in the place of cash or its equivalent. A capital gain or loss may result from the sale or exchange of a property.

• **Holding Period for Property.** The holding period of a property is the term of ownership from the date it is acquired until the date sold. The holding period determines if the gain upon sale is a short or long-term gain. Thus, the holding period can have a significant impact on the taxable capital gain created (IRC 1202).

Gain from the sale of property held for one year or less is a short-term capital gain. Gain from the sale of property held over one year is a long-term capital gain. This means, if a property is sold on the one-year anniversary date its acquisition the capital gain will be short term. If the property is sold the day after the anniversary date of the date it was acquired the capital gain is long term. The applicable tax rates can produce a major variance in taxes due.

• **Basis.** The basis of a property is the cost paid for the property in cash or the market value of other property given in the event of an exchange. Basis can also include costs incurred to acquire and improve the property so it is suitable for use.

• **Realized Gain or Loss from the Sale of Property.** A gain is realized when a sale of a property occurs and there is a difference between the net sales price and the basis. The total of cash and other property (at market value) received is used to determine the amount realized. Subtract basis from the amount realized to determine if a gain or loss occurs. Realized gains or losses do not occur with changes in the market value of a property. A sale or exchange triggers a realized gain.

• **Installment Sale Method.** For many years sellers have enjoyed the benefits of seller financing to support their retirement objectives. With a modest down payment monthly income can be received over several years. This is called the "installment sale" method of business disposition. It was also a tax efficient strategy. Capital gains taxes were due only as payments were collected. This changed due to changes in the tax code that were enacted in December 1999.

An installment sale as defined by the IRC 7355 is, "a sale of property where at least one payment for the property is received after the year in which the sale occurs." Even a sale of property that is paid for in a lump sum can be an installment sale if the lump-sum payment is received in a tax year that follows the year of sale. When sellers finance their property they typically take from 20% to 40% of the purchase price as a down payment and "carry the balance" over a reasonable amount of time. This is an installment sale.

Favorable tax treatment was offered because a portion of the gross profit from the installment sale (profit in excess of basis) is included in the seller's income each year in which a payment for the property is received. As a result the taxpayer uses this installment method for reporting gross profit from qualifying installment sales. The amount of gross profit is not affected, however. This method only extends the time over which gross profit is received as taxable income. Therefore, the installment method permits payments of taxes due on the gross profit or capital gain to be deferred into years following the year when the sale occurred.

Controversy has erupted over new tax legislation enacted and effective December 17, 1999. President Bill Clinton signed the Ticket to Work and Work Incentives Improvement Act. Unfortunately, this act inadvertently affected installment sales [under most conditions] for business owners planning to sell their business. Those conditions pertain to taxpayers using the accrual-basis of accounting. For them, payment of the taxes on the gross profit or gain [that might have been paid over several years] is due in one lump sum during the first year of the sale *regardless of when payments are received.*

The effect of the law does not render use of the cash flow method of valuation inoperable. Quite the opposite. This method becomes the best way to determine value when bank financing is involved. However, an estimated 200,000 small businesses that are sold each year will be adversely affected by this new IRS regulation. That is because, in order to pay the costs to sell a business, plus all the taxes due, financial leverage created by seller financing is lost. Sellers will demand cash in full. Since the lending requirements of banks are more strict business prices will fall. Some estimates suggest prices will fall by as much as 20%. In fact, many viable service companies with limited tangible assets can become attractive only at fire sale prices.

Fortunately, floods of concern from proponents of small business have brought this egregious legislation to the attention of Washington lawmakers. Prior to publication of the *Business Valuation Bluebook* a bill to repeal this controversial provision, S. 2005 in the United States Senate has been referred to the Senate Finance Committee for consideration. A similar bill, the Small Business Tax Fairness Act, quickly moved through the U.S. House of Representatives and was passed by the House March 9, 2000. This act includes a provision to repeal the new installment-sales tax law, which affects owners who sell their businesses using the installment sale method. The Small Business Tax Fairness Act is expected to pass the Senate also. President Clinton's response to signing this Act into law is not known at the time of publication of this book. Check with appropriate counsel before using the installment sales method of selling a business.

• **Tax-Deferred Exchanges.** IRC 1031 states "No gain or loss shall be recognized on the exchange of property held for productive use in a trade or business or for investment if such property is exchanged solely for property of like kind which is to be held either for productive use in a trade or business or for investment."

• **Like-Kind.** Where properties exchanged are considered to be like kind, held for productive use in a trade, business or for an investment, no gain is recognized.

Treasury Regulations state the words "like kind" refer to the nature or character of the property and not to grade or quality. Like kind exchanges in real estate may occur between apartments, industrial buildings, commercial land for development or farmland for use in a business.

- **Three-Party Exchanges.** Many times an investor will not want to sell a property because the cost of capital gains taxes are unacceptable. A tax-deferred exchange can be a good strategy to use if a second party with a like-kind property can be found. The two exchange investment properties. If not, a third party may become involved.

In a three-party exchange a third party agrees to buy a property available only through a tax deferred exchange. Title of the property available for exchange passes to the new buyer. A qualified intermediary holds money received in the exchange. The seller locates an investment property for sale that would have qualified as a like-kind exchange with the original property sold. The intermediary purchases the property and delivers title to the original selling party. A non-simultaneous tax-deferred exchange has occurred.

- **Non-Simultaneous Exchanges.** The Tax Reform Act of 1984 provides that a non-simultaneous exchange is a like-kind exchange if it adheres to the following rules. The buyer must identify the property they elect to acquire within 45 days from the transfer date of the property sold. They must take ownership within the lesser of 180 days from the transfer date of the property sold or the date a tax return is filed for the year in which the transfer of the original property sold occurred.

- **Boot.** Cash or non like-kind property received in excess of the fair market value of property relinquished in a tax-deferred exchange. Boot is created when the values of the properties exchanged are not equal which is often the case. To the extent that boot is received a gain is recognized.

- **Related-Party Exchanges.** Sometimes there are tax benefits created when related parties exchange properties. One such benefit occurs when the larger gain on one property is shifted onto another with a lower tax applicable tax rate. If either party sells or disposes of the property received within two years of the exchange date the original exchange will not be treated as like kind.

Business Expenses And Deductions

• **Nature of Business Expenses.** IRC 1652 and 212 discuss what types of expenses may be deductible for business purposes. Generally, acceptable business expenses are those that support of profit motivated activity. They may be deducted from business income provided they are well documented, not unreasonable, consistent with the business activity, and necessary to insure continued business operations.

• **Depreciation.** IRC 167 refers to depreciation while Sec. 167 and 168 refer to depreciation and cost recovery. These are the periodic write-off, or deduction, of an asset used in a business or investment, which is held for the production of income. The term of depreciation that applies to various types of assets can vary widely.

The depreciation recovery period for real property that was placed in service after 1986 is 27.5 years for residential rental property and 39 years for non-residential real property. Tangible personal property is divided into classes. These are 3-year, 5-year, 7-year, 10-year, 15-year and 20-year.

Two methods to calculate the amount of depreciation taken exist. Generally, the method of depreciation taken is determined by the year the property was placed in service. Rules regarding depreciation schedules have changed. After 1986 an accelerated method may be used for personal tangible property but may be converted to the straight-line method when it yields a larger amount. A straight-line method divides the amount that can be depreciated by the number of years in the applicable depreciation period to determine annual depreciation deductions.

• **Intangibles-Amortization.** Businesses are allowed to deduct an expense called amortization. This is the write-off of intangible assets, which is comparable to depreciation or cost recovery for tangible property. Intangible assets are written-off over a wide variety of terms but always on a straight-line basis. IRC 197 pertains to the amortization deductions that may be taken for intangibles purchased including goodwill; start-up expenses are covered under IRC 195 and organizational expenses are covered under IRC 195.

Types of intangibles include goodwill, covenants not to compete, franchises, trademarks, trade names, licenses, permits or granted rights such as a broadcast license, copyrights, patents, secret formulas or production methods, competitive intelligence. These assets are deemed to add value to a business.

• **Taxes.** Certain types of taxes may be deducted for purposes of calculating federal income taxes. Some examples of taxes that may be deducted are State, local and foreign property taxes paid and taxes paid in the operation of a business or trade for purposes of producing income. Certain types of personal property taxes are deductible as well.

A few examples of taxes that are not deductible include: Federal income taxes, inheritance taxes, gift taxes, import duties, employer social security contributions, state and local sales taxes or state inheritance and gift taxes.

• **Travel.** Travel expenses are costs incurred by a taxpayer that occur while they are "away from home" and working to further the objectives of their business or employment activity. Qualifying travel expenses may be deducted from income. A non-deductible 2% floor may apply based on reimbursement of expenses to the taxpayer. IRC 274 discusses the specific rules that can affect the deductibility of travel expenses.

• **Transportation.** Transportation expenses are generally regarded as travel expenses incurred in the normal course of business while the taxpayer is not away from home.

• **Entertainment/Meals.** Deductibility of entertainment and meals expenses are covered under IRC 162 and 212. Taking a client to the baseball game or dinner in a five-star restaurant is impressive for one while enjoyable for the other. Enforcement problems have developed. IRC 274 disallows certain entertainment expenses and provides rules that classify, restrict and set standards for record keeping. The reason for clarification in Sec. 274 is while business entertainment can be an important business practice the benefit may also inure to the taxpayer.

In addition, any expense for entertainment or meals is subject to a 50% disallowance. The deduction available is the actual cost of entertainment and meals including beverages and tips and taxes when reduced by one half. This is the amount that can be deducted for qualifying business entertainment and meal expenses.

• **Home Office Expenses.** In 1997 the Taxpayer Relief Act made it possible for home-based entrepreneurs and telecommuters to deduct more expenses related to performing their work from an office in their home.

A person working in their home uses a portion of it for the purposes of producing business income. This qualifies them to receive a deduction on the assets (or portion of assets) in the home that are used. It can be difficult, however, to determine the amount of deduction that may be taken.

To qualify as business-related expenses from the home, one of the following conditions must be present. The home office is used by the taxpayer for any of their trade, professional or business activities; a meeting location for clients, patients or customers; or if the home office used is not attached to the home itself. Employers must also prove the home office is for the benefit of the taxpayer or employer.

Expenses deducted will include those directly related to the office that those which are indirectly related. Direct expenses are decorating costs. Indirect expenses are those that are inherent in the cost of the property and would be calculated as a prorated share of the total. Property taxes, insurance, interest, utilities, repairs, and etc., are examples. For additional details describing the amount of deduction that may be taken see IRC 280.

• **Interest.** Interest is the cost businesses pay for the use of money. This includes loan points and fees, finance charges, and premiums. Interest was described in Chapter Five as part of the cost of financial leverage in a business transaction. Interest incurred on behalf of the business activity, mortgage or otherwise, is deductible in full from business income.

Appendix D
General Terms and Features of Acquisitions

The following is intended for general information purposes only. Laws governing small business acquisitions and dispositions change periodically. State laws affecting these issues vary widely. This material is not to be considered legal, accounting or tax advice. Readers are strongly advised to speak with their respective legal, accounting or tax consultants before attempting to employ any of the information or concepts stated herein.

Acquisition Agreement

When the buyer and seller reach an agreement to sell, by the basic structure of this transaction (terms and conditions) a written acquisition agreement should be prepared. Generally buyers prepare the initial acquisition agreement since it is they who are advancing an offer.

Many acquisition agreements are prepared on a standard form. These can be effective provided they meet all the needs of parties involved. Many do not. However, most will share the same elements, which are listed here.

- Identity of assets or stock to be sold, the price and terms, and the mechanics or rules governing the transaction
- Other conditions of the agreement including, but not limited to, amount of earnest money or deposit delivered with the acquisition agreement, financing, provisions for a covenant not to compete, training to be provided by the seller; earn out provisions, etc.

- Representations and warranties of the seller (e.g., where real estate is included, the seller may warrant title to the property is good and marketable)
- Representations and warranties of the buyer
- Covenants pending a closing
- Conditions precedent to a closing
- Provisions of the closing or termination of the agreement (e.g., setting the time and place of closing, form of funds to be brought to the closing, etc.; also, may include a penalty for failure to close when all other conditions of the agreement have been satisfied – is often forfeiture of a percentage of the sales price, which may be taken from the deposit
- Indemnifications of the parties involved (buyer to seller, seller to buyer, both to lender, their professional representatives, etc.)
- Provision of payment for fees, expenses and other miscellaneous matters

Acquisition of Assets vs. Stock

Many small businesses are closely held. This means they have small number of owners or are family owned. They may be incorporated, too.

When acquiring a business that has been incorporated, most buyers prefer to acquire the assets from the corporation or partnership instead of the stock in the legal entity. This occurs because the company, not its stockholders, owns the business assets. The stockholders own stock in the company. Here are two important reasons.

When acquiring assets, buyers establish a new value for depreciable tangible and intangible assets being purchased. It may be larger than the property's basis under current ownership. The new greater value increases the amount of depreciation or amortization that may be taken by a buyer. This often compares favorably to the remaining tax benefit available to the corporation that owns the assets.

Also, there may be certain liabilities that accompany ownership of a corporation. These may be outstanding financial obligations or existing and potential liabilities created by lawsuits. These can pass to a buyer as the new owner of stock in the company.

To avoid unintended assumption of liabilities and establish a new basis for depreciation of assets, buyers often elect to buy business assets rather than outstanding stock.

Allocation of Price

The sale of a business involves the sale of tangible and intangible assets. The total of all property acquired is the purchase price. The purpose of the allocation is to establish a new basis for depreciation and amortization based on the fair market value of the property involved.

As a condition precedent to closing, a value must be placed on each asset acquired – both tangible and intangible. Both parties must agree to the allocation, which can have varying tax consequences for each. Allocation should be done by the parties tax consultant or other qualified professional representatives. The Internal Revenue Service has the authority to review allocations it considers unreasonable.

Appraisal

As a condition precedent to a closing, a property appraisal is often requested to confirm value. A buyer, seller or lender providing financing to the buyer acquiring property may require this. Payment for the appraisal may be negotiated between the parties. In those cases where a business acquisition is contemplated, business valuation skill on the part of the buyer or lender will be most helpful. The supply of qualified business appraisers is small to nonexistent in rural areas.

Approvals

Prior to closing many approvals may be needed. These are conditions precedent to a closing. Typical approvals needed for most acquisitions are approval of licensing or franchising authorities; approval of lender for financing; approval of buyers or their professional representative's review of financials and all other aspects of the business operation and its operating agreements; approval of the buyer's financial qualifications where seller financing is involved; and approval of stockholder where necessary.

As a general rule it is best to secure as many approvals as possible prior to the closing. This prevents last minute changes that can often occur.

Assumption of Debt

Many times a business sold will have existing debt. Buyers may elect to assume the debt and, if so, should state the terms and conditions under which this may occur. Various questions should be considered. If these are to be renegotiated, when is this to be completed? Will the seller's guarantee be released or not? Is the buyer given permission to discuss the outstanding debt with the appropriate creditors?

In other instances, the buyer may want to acquire a business free and clear of debts liens and encumbrances of any kind. Normally this is more to a buyer's liking and is especially preferred where a lender is providing acquisition financing. In such cases the agreement will discuss the nature, size and terms of outstanding business debts together with a condition that they will be paid in full at closing.

Assumption of Agreements

A condition that provides for a buyer's assumption of agreements usually refers to a franchise agreement. It may also include special arrangements with business vendors or professionals representing the business whose involvement is to be continued. These would be noted in the acquisition agreement.

Bill of Sale

A bill of sale is evidence a transfer of personal property has occurred. Because real estate is not included in the sale of many businesses, a bill of sales is a common form of conveyance. Where real estate is included, conveyance is by way of a deed.

Bulk Sales Law

Many states have a bulk sales law. This is commonly applied to transactions where an inventory for resale is included in the sale. The bulk sales provisions require that notification be given to a business's creditors prior to the sale of property or a business where credit has been extended. As a result the creditor can make claims for payment prior to the closing.

The intended result of a bulk sales law is to draw a line between debts of the buyer and the seller. Creditors are paid from the rightful debtor, and a business is conveyed without debts except for those a buyer assumes and agrees to pay. In some states a Uniform Commercial Code provision provides for payment of creditors out of sales proceeds.

A problem with the bulk sales law occurs among buyers and sellers who do not want to notify creditors of a sale, thus losing confidentiality. This can be of particular concern to a seller where a closing remains in doubt. Buyers, on the other hand, do not want outstanding debts to surface as claims against them – the new owner of the business. Even when the buyer is not responsible for payment, creditors have been known to refuse delivery of additional merchandise until outstanding claims are paid by prior ownership or anyone else.

As a compromise, some buyers and sellers circumvent the bulk sales provisions. The seller gives the buyer a list of outstanding business debts as of the closing and agrees to pay them from closing proceeds. Thereafter, he or she may be willing to escrow additional closing proceeds for a short time. These can be used to pay of other undisclosed debts if any are discovered. If none exist, escrowed funds are released to the seller. As an additional provision the seller may agree to indemnify and hold the buyer harmless for any liabilities incurred from creditor claims that originated prior to the closing.

Covenants Pending a Closing

These are items that restrict or obligate buyer and seller to avoid taking, or to take, certain actions prior to the closing. Restricting the release of information to parties to the transaction and their professional representatives might be one example. Other covenants might require the sellers to continue normal business operations, conducting no unusual activities such as a going-out-of-business sales; to keep the negotiations strictly confidential; to keep the business property well maintained and insured; and to make timely payment of all taxes and financial obligations prior to closing.

Covenant Not to Compete

A covenant not to compete, or non-competition agreement, is generally given from a seller to a buyer. It is important when the seller possesses technical knowledge about the business being purchased that could be used by a competitor to attract their market share of business. The result would be a reduction of revenue and performance created by the seller's actions after a closing.

Most covenants not to compete include four key provisions: a term, a geographic reference, the type of activity not permitted and a value. There may be other conditions, too, including remedies for violation of the covenant.

Conditions Precedent to Closing

Actions a buyer or seller must, or must not do to accomplish an activity are conditions precedent to a closing. For example, buyers or their professional representatives must review and approve of the business financials within 10 business days from the date the acquisition agreement is fully executed. Here is a partial list of the topics that might be included as a condition, that is to be performed or subject to review and approval. Note the list is by no means complete and could include many other conditions that might pertain to a unique buyer or business situation.

- Financing commitment
- Appraisal of property
- Financial statements review
- Business operations review
- Due diligence
- Training or training plan for buyer
- Credit, financial and qualifications of buyer
- Business, franchise and professional service agreements
- Review of customer and vendor lists
- Approvals from licensing and regulatory authorities
- Completed physical inventory and approval
- Review of all tangibles and intangibles
- Review of debt and liabilities assumed
- Bulk sales compliance
- Sales tax treatment of inventory purchased
- Certificate of good standing and all other documentation

Earnest Money

When arranging transactions to sell and buy businesses and/or real estate, the ability to keep a transaction from falling apart is often related to the amount of earnest money placed on deposit by a buyer. When a substantial earnest money deposit is made, the buyer is more committed to perform. In such instances a seller is also more willing to take the buyer seriously than if a promissory note or a dollar bill is clipped to an offer.

Receipt and use of earnest money is a negotiable issue. It may be delivered in one or more installments. These can begin at the first execution date of the acquisition agreement and continue as conditions are completed in an orderly sequence. Earnest money may be refundable if certain conditions precedent to a closing remains unfulfilled by closing or a certain date stated earlier. However, certain expenses, such as appraisal fees, may be deducted from the earnest money. In other instances, where conditions are fully executed, the earnest money is credited to the purchase price of the property.

Earn Outs

An earn out is a form of payment buyers offer sellers where there is uncertainty about the future performance of a business. To implement an earn-out strategy, the buyer will acquire the business and agree to pay additional premiums to the seller based on business results received. A simple form of earn out would be where the seller receives a small percentage of the increase in business revenue. If the results improve, the selling party is rewarded. If results decline, no additional payment is made.

Earn outs are a good way to test a seller's confidence in the future of a business. It is also helpful to keep a seller committed to work for the continued success of the enterprise. There is a direct financial incentive for this support.

Expiration of Offers

An expiration of offer occurs when the acquisition agreement includes a date by which a response from the seller is required. If none is received the offer is withdrawn. Buyers often place expiration dates in acquisition offers to encourage a timely response from sellers. If none is given, they move on. Sometimes they are used to pressure a seller into quick acceptance. This tactic is unhelpful because it usually results in a seller's avoidance of the offer entirely, or their attachment of additional provisions that have a nullifying effect on the expiration date. The seller's response may also be accompanied by an equally short deadline for the buyer's acceptance of added provisions.

An expiration of offer that provides a seller with a reasonable amount of time to consider the proposition is an acceptable approach. Such an expiration should be included to prevent sellers from considering the offer indefinitely and attempting to find other offers that are better. Also, a reasonable expiration date, helps ensure the buyer's proposal is not accepted at later time after which the buyer has made an investment elsewhere.

Financing

Since most buyers of businesses want to use investment leverage in acquisitions, a condition providing them with a chance to secure a financing commitment is frequently included in acquisition agreements.

Buyers often state very specific terms of financing requested. Sellers counter by adjusting them to reflect outside limits. For example, a seller might modify the buyer's statement of terms that seek financing at 9% annual interest rate to financing that does not exceed 10%. The difference is the buyer could use a commitment of financing at 8.5% as a device to avoid the contract *for any other reason*. The seller's approach would eliminate this loophole.

In general, when securing financing is a condition precedent to closing, the terms stated are amount, interest rate, loan term, method of payment, collateral and personal guarantees involved.

Future Business Assurances

Occasionally buyers ask sellers to state they know of no events occurring or about to occur that could negatively affect business performance. This is not an unreasonable condition. Sellers respond, however, by stating they are delivering the business "as is" and no warranties for future performance are made or implied.

This is an important issue since the earnings reconstruction used in a business valuation process is designed to reveal the differences between taxable income and cash flow. As such it is not a tool to forecast the future. It is an indication of what has been and is based entirely on trailing earnings. For this reason, sellers creating a value range based on next year's cash flow are well advised to keep their cash flow forecasts to themselves. If desired, buyers should construct these with the help of their professional representatives.

More importantly, when a final or year-end financial statement is to be received between a letter of intent or acquisition agreement and closing, it is unwise to link approval of the business's financial condition to receipt of these documents. They could reveal a dramatic downturn in business. It is better to state the business results should reflect no change in business revenue or improvements that can be defined.

Good Standing of Corporation

States require corporations to pay what is commonly called a "franchise tax." This accompanies the ability of an entity to legally operate and conduct lawful business in the state in which it is licensed to operate.

A certificate of good standing is a statement from regulatory authorities to indicate a corporation is in compliance, taxes are paid and the entity is in "good standing." This certificate is often requested as a condition precedent to a closing. It ensures the corporation selling assets has the authority to act.

Indemnification

This is a condition whereby the parties to an agreement agree to compensate the other for damages or losses that may occur. In an acquisition agreement the sellers would indemnify buyers against any losses that might occur as a result of debts not assumed by the buyer and unpaid by the seller.

How might this occur? Suppose a liquor store changes hands July 1 and the seller fails to pay an outstanding invoice for beer delivered. The new owner places an order for more stock to be received by July 3. The vendor refuses to deliver until the outstanding invoice is paid. The loss of sales can be substantial, and under certain conditions the buyer might have a claim.

Pending litigation and undisclosed liabilities are common reasons a seller will indemnify a buyer. Brokers guiding a business transaction often state in the acquisition agreement that they have made no representations. They further state that execution of the agreement by the parties is their agreement to indemnify the broker against consequences of the transaction.

Inspections

Inspections may be a condition precedent to closing. Approvals often accompany the inspections as well as a date by which approval is to be received. Handled in this way the inspections are gradually removed and no longer a roadblock to closing.

Inspections may occur for many reasons, including business financials; agreements such as including leases, franchises, employment contracts, professional service agreements, etc.; business property, including real estate and improvements, furnishings, fixtures and equipment; and operating procedures.

Intangibles

Property that contributes to business performance but cannot be touched or felt is intangible property. Covenants not to compete, goodwill, customer lists and a franchise are common forms of intangible assets. The acquisition agreement should state the intangibles acquired together with allocated values.

Inventory

Acquisition agreements for the purchase of a retail business will state as a condition precedent to closing the inventory must be counted just prior to closing. This provision will often name the service to perform the inventory and to govern the process. Both buyer and seller should be present at the inventory to approve of the process. Buyers many want to exclude certain types of inventory that appear damaged or dated.

When taking an inventory for most small businesses, the easiest method to use involves categorizing all merchandise by markup. For example, all merchandise in one category is marked up 30%, items in another category are marked up 40% and the rest is marked up 20%. Merchandise is counted at its retail value. Divide the total by 1.00 plus the percent of markup to identify actual cost of the merchandise. This is a simple and generally accepted way to determine the value of inventory that will be included with the business at the closing, which should follow immediately.

When offered for sale, a business may be priced plus or including inventory at seller's cost. The difference can be meaningful when attempting to attract a buyer. One price is much lower but more uncertain; the other is higher but instills more confidence in the buyer. Using the latter, if the inventory at closing is less than the amount stated to be present in the acquisition agreement, the price is adjusted accordingly. If the amount of inventory is greater, the buyer may pay the added amount, issue a credit to the seller for merchandise in the future or add the additional amount to seller financing if applicable.

Letter of Intent

A letter of intent may be used as a precedent to an acquisition agreement. A buyer prepares a letter of intent, signs it and delivers it to the seller, who signs it, too. The letter of intent is executed prior to a formal acquisition agreement.

Letters of intent are helpful when there is a need to reduce a basic agreement between buyer and seller to writing. This prevents future misunderstanding and helps avoid renegotiation. Also, a letter of intent conveys a moral commitment between the parties. To the extent that business people keep their word, a letter of intent is helpful to move a transaction along.

Letters of intent generally have several common elements:

- A statement of whether the letter of intent is binding or not
- A statement of whether a formal acquisition agreement will be prepared, in which case the letter of intent is subject to that document's execution
- The form of the transaction: is it an asset purchase, the purchase of a business with or without real estate,

or a purchase of company stock?
- The price and terms
- Significant provisions, covenants and conditions precedent to execution of the acquisition agreement and/or a closing

For obvious reasons, letters of intent are also helpful to use when it is expected the time until an acquisition agreement is executed will be lengthy.

Limitation of Liability

One way entrepreneurs attempt to reduce exposure created by indemnifications is to establish an upper limit on their liability. This may be a reasonable request provided the limit is established at an appropriate level. Some feel their liability should not exceed the value of property conveyed. Others feel the limit should be tied to historical limits if they exist. In any case, when limitations on liability are introduced, the other party is given a reason for added concern.

Also, when indemnity is given to prevent liability, parties attempt to secure joint and several liabilities. Normally this occurs when more than one individual is liable for an obligation. When used, all individuals are each liable for the entire obligation – it is not based on their prorated share of the obligation. Thus, collection is easier because it is presumed certain members of a group who are jointly and severally liable will encourage full payment from the entire group.

Misrepresentation

Buyers and sellers make statements about themselves and their businesses to each other. When it is discovered (usually by a due diligence or background check) that something has been omitted that should not have been, a misrepresentation may have occurred.

The severity of misrepresentations is often determined by the intent or non-intent to omit information and whether it is material to the terms and conditions of the acquisition agreement or not. Where a misrepresentation is intentional and material, a buyer's typical recourse is to walk away from the transaction. If the transaction has already occurred, a buyer's recourse may include other legal remedies.

Physical Condition of Fixed Assets

As a condition precedent to closing a buyer may want assurances the physical condition of all property purchased is in good working condition. Inspections are typical for real estate, and this may require wording to allow professional inspectors access to the property for the purpose of making specific inspections. These are often at the buyer's expense. A provision may be inserted into the agreement to resolve any dispute arising from assets found to be in poor condition.

Representations

These are statements a seller usually makes to a buyer that indicate the condition of a business being acquired. They often refer to other statements – the financials of the business – and are subject to verification. Representations are normally tied to a date that has already passed. Changes since then are the subject of additional disclosures.

Right of Recision

Acquisition agreements for a small business may include a right of recision for the buyer. This means that within a specified period of time, usually determined by state statues, the buyer may elect to cancel the agreement. The term in which a right of recision may be exercised is usually short, 24 to 48 hours.

Sales Taxes

When the form of acquisition is an asset purchase, it may be necessary to state certain provisions to describe the purchase of inventory. This can be necessary because if improperly done, or omitted, a buyer purchasing inventory could be liable for payment of sales taxes on the entire amount purchased. It can be substantial. Because sales taxes are affected by state and local regulations, the buyer should investigate this carefully with local authorities.

Tangibles

Tangibles are the property being conveyed that has physical form and substance. This includes real property but more specifically refers to personal property such as business furnishings, fixtures, equipment, leasehold improvements and inventory. The acquisition agreement should allocate a reasonable value to each tangible asset conveyed in the transaction. This value normally becomes the basis used to calculate the amount of depreciation a buyer will receive in the future and the amount of gain a seller will receive from the sale.

Training

Another provision of the acquisition agreement requires the seller train the buyer in all aspects of business operations. When used, the amount and term of training should be specified. Also, sellers often receive compensation for their involvement. The acquisition agreement should indicate if this compensation is to be considered income or a part of the price paid for the business.

About the Author

Chad Simmons is an entrepreneur, author and small business columnist.

In 1979 Mr. Simmons began a real estate career with United Farm Agency, the nations largest country real estate franchiser where he focused on the sale of businesses in the rural sector. By 1984 he had received nearly all the company's national sales awards for outstanding performance. In the process he became an expert in small business valuation as well as a franchisee for the company. In 1986 he was hired as the sales manager for the franchiser and advanced rapidly through several positions. He culminated his United career by becoming President, CEO and one of its major stockholders.

Mr. Simmons has taught business valuation throughout the U.S. for 15 years. His seminar and workshop text, *Rule of Thumb: The Standard in Pricing Small Businesses*, are popular among entrepreneurs, real estate brokers, agents and related business professionals. The *Business Valuation Bluebook* is a derivative of that work.

After forming The Corinth Press in 1996 Mr. Simmons published his first book, *The Anonymous Entrepreneur*. A study of the entrepreneurial attitude it illustrates how state of mind is a key reason for many entrepreneurs' success. Mr. Simmons also writes *The Entrepreneurial Attitude*, a regular column for small business news publications. His comments illustrate ways the entrepreneurial attitude contributes to success.

Mr. Simmons consults with emerging entrepreneurs and business professionals who want to sell or buy business properties. He helps them identify and overcome growth walls,

develop marketing themes and appeals, supervise sales processes, and build and execute plans to manage results that follow.
He also owns and manages Simmons Investment Company,
LLC, a firm that invests in equities, real estate and small businesses.

Mr. Simmons lives in Leawood, Kansas, with his family and
enjoys the diversity and rewards of an entrepreneurial lifestyle.

Notes

Notes